MAGIC IN HERBS

Harvesting Sweet Basil at the Weathered Oak Herb Farm, on Bradley Hills, Bethesda, Maryland

MAGIC IN HERBS

BY LEONIE DE SOUNIN

With an Introduction by Miriam Birdseye
Extension Nutritionist, United States Department of Agriculture

GRAMERCY PUBLISHING COMPANY • NEW YORK

This edition published by Gramercy Publishing Company,
a division of Crown Publishers, Inc.,
by arrangement with William Morrow & Company, Inc.
d e f g h

DESIGNED BY STEFAN SALTER

Manufactured in the United States of America

My deep gratitude goes to Ruth S-B. Feis, my collaborating editor, who with an admirable understanding helped to shape my ideas to a clear picture of what I was desirous to convey. Her kindness and patience during many months of intense work together is unforgettable to me, as is her encouragement and her always joyful coöperation. This book probably would never have been published without her keen perception of its value and her enthusiasm for its subject.

LEONIE DE SOUNIN

CONTENTS

LIST OF ILLUSTRATIONS

ILLUSTRATIONS COURTESY OF
THE UNITED STATES DEPARTMENT OF AGRICULTURE

INTRODUCTION

As THE AUTHOR'S FIRST and most devoted disciple in working magic on everyday meals through the understanding use of herbs, I am happy that this book will bring to a wide circle of herb-lovers, present and prospective, the experience, the enthusiasm, the discriminating judgment, and some at least of the fascinating background, of this remarkable woman who has guided me and many others into high culinary adventure.

Men and women who do their own streamlined cooking; hostesses in search of distinguished yet economical menus; travelers who cherish the memory of haunting flavors which they have never quite succeeded in reproducing; home economists wishing to add the subtle art of seasoning to their mastery of the scientific principles of cooking; teachers of advanced cooking and institutional management; extension workers who have already aroused some interest in using herbs; armchair cooks who somehow absorb culinary delights from the written page—all these and many more will peruse the pages of

Magic in Herbs with pleasure and profit. With pleasure, for this book is written in the charming style of an experienced writer of stories and plays. With profit, because it makes a baffling subject plain, and throws sidelights on details of culinary management of which many American homemakers are abysmally ignorant.

It is not exaggeration, I think, to claim that in the ten years in which Leonie de Sounin and I have lived together, my respect and admiration for my friend's culinary achievements have continued to increase. So has my realization that she is a woman of many gifts and varied contacts, a keen observer of human nature, an inimitable *raconteuse,* a stimulating friend.

After several years together we began seriously to work on herbs. The crusade to restore the use of herbs to its rightful place in the scheme of fine and simple living was just gathering headway in America, and I wanted to bring to rural women, through the Cooperative Extension Service of the United States Department of Agriculture and the State Agricultural Colleges, the joys of a fragrant herb garden and adventures with new yet age-old flavor combinations, as a tiny but heart-warming part of our important live-at-home program. So I needed to learn everything I could about growing and using herbs.

In our garden apartment shut in by blossoming shrubs

and vines we had the "makings" for such a piece of work—a flagged patio bordered by miniature flower beds, a tiny but complete kitchen laboratory, a charming dining-room in which to regale our friends. We planned to make the most of these advantages.

Fortune guided us to Mrs. Florence Bratenahl, first president of the Herb Society of America, who had just opened an herb garden for the sale of dried herbs and growing plants. We made our selection with her advice and soon our patio border rejoiced in lusty plants of thyme, marjoram, basils of several varieties, rosemary, tarragon, the summer and winter savories, together with chervil and chive, and dill grown from seed.

The first dish I begged for was the *omelette aux fines herbes* which had intrigued me years before when traveling on the Continent but which, try as I might, I had never been able to re-create.

Day by day my education progressed as herbs fresh and dried appeared in soups, in sauces, in salads; with meats, fish and fowl. Soon I knew the fragrance and flavor of each tiny leaf and could even untangle subtle herb combinations.

I enticed visiting extension workers to our little apartment on the hill, to share with them the new interest and graciousness which were being added to my own living, and kindle in them the zeal to hand these on to the rural women whom they teach. For these well-trained workers, Leonie de Sounin took delight in planning simple, delicious menus and purposely inexpensive menus to illustrate the various uses of herbs. We preceded these meals by a personally conducted tour of our pocket-handkerchief herb bed and a personal introduction to the characters in the impending herb drama.

The many small herb gardens which have sprung up in the footsteps of extension workers the country over, testify to the effectiveness of this combination of seeing, sniffing, tasting and discussing, with which we sought to inspire our prospective missionaries. Leonie de Sounin deserves the lion's share of the credit for what was accomplished. Failure to provide the directions for using the herbs was the weak link in our chain. You can understand, therefore, how I rejoice that these directions and recipes appear in the present volume.

In selecting and shaping the material for her book the author has experimented with others than myself. These others were interested married women who made up the informal and phenomenally successful demonstration groups frequently mentioned in the text. The things these pupils wanted to know, the questions she found they needed to have answered, the directions and recipes she wrote down for them have all been crystallized for the benefit of other beginners in the pages of *Magic in Herbs.*

This book is not only exceptionally authoritative and readable, it is also a timely and effective contribution to the renaissance of an art that in our own country, for a time at least, suffered almost total eclipse. In the early days, women coming from other lands brought with them the knowledge of growing and using herbs developed by long practice under the watchful eyes of their mothers. Wherever they settled, they planted herb gardens and cherished them. Many of us still associate the sun-drenched peace and fragrance of such gardens with childhood visits to our grandmothers. But the mobility of homes and break-up of families that went with the exploitation of a continent, the mingling of racial cultures by marriage, the adoption of "American ways" to please the children, the herding of population in cities, and the developments of industry, commerce, even of education, gradually obliterated from the minds of average Americans the memory and the appreciation of anything so subtle and so individual as the art of seasoning with herbs. Today children leave the home to learn, and mothers leave it to earn. Where, in this modern scheme, is the institution for training teachers of home economics, which maintains a well-planned, fragrant herb garden, so that in addition to grounding its students in the science of cooking, it can give them a skill and enthusiasm for the art of seasoning, which can give distinction to the most inexpensive dish?

The Herb Society of America was formed some years ago with the motto "For Use and For Delight". The growing membership and varied activities of this organization, composed as it is of those who have made substantial contribution to the movement, give evidence that real progress is being made. So does the lengthening list of small concerns that raise and market dried herbs and herb blends of good quality, and growing plants. Heartening indeed is the increasing number of well-written books which give real guidance in using herbs in cooking, and the number of men and women who are adding accent and variety to everyday meals by the discriminating use of herbs.

But alas, teachers with background, experience and conviction are still few and far between.

Leonie de Sounin is such a teacher. *Magic in Herbs* sets forth her teaching.

MIRIAM BIRDSEYE,
Extension Nutritionist,
United States Department of Agriculture

Washington, D. C.
September, 1941

Perennials blooming in early May at the Weathered Oak Herb Farm.
Left to right: Winter Savory, Lemon Balm, Nepeta Mussini, Rue.
Nepeta is used for borders.

The "Fines Herbes" and Chive.
Left to right: Chive, Sweet Marjoram, Summer Savory, Sweet Basil, Chervil, Tarragon (spray in foreground).

A delicate combination for an OMELETTE AUX FINES HERBES. *Chive, Summer Savory, Thyme, Chervil.*

Another good OMELETTE *combination: Chive, Sweet Marjoram, Summer Savory, Chervil.*

A good mixture for tomato salad: Chive, Summer Savory, Sweet Basil, Chervil.

Chive blooms the second spring against a lusty plant of Chamomile.

Chive wears a lavender crown the second spring (biennial).

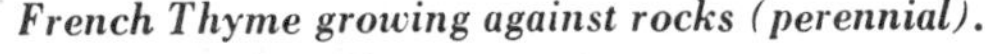

French Thyme growing against rocks (perennial).

French Sorrel blooms early (perennial).

Winter Savory blooms all summer and late into the fall.

Four Basils–Compact, Purple, Sweet, and Dwarf Purple.

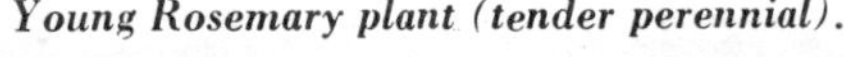

Young Rosemary plant (tender perennial).

Harvesting Summer Savory at the Weathered Oak Herb Farm.
The growing tips are cut just as the buds are about to open, for at this time the aromatic oils that give the plant its characteristic fragrance and flavor are at their strongest.

A bed of Mints in full bloom.

MAGIC IN HERBS

CHAPTER ONE

Introducing Myself

WHEN I DECIDED TO WRITE THIS BOOK on my experience with and knowledge of herbs and how to use them, I began to delve into old family papers which reached back to my childhood. Memories of those golden days became visions of the past. Our old castle, a castle of the venerable age of three centuries, was in the wonderfully fertile land of the Moravian-Slovakian part of former Bohemia. We all belonged to the Austrian Empire, which throughout my early life was a most peaceful country of a noble culture and civilization with a very happy populace. It was a friendly white castle with green shutters—a comfortable horseshoe building with a prominent front—superb hand-wrought high iron fences and a gate which first had to be opened from the inside to let the world in. But there was an entrance at the back, the friendliest, most simple approach, with no gates, but an alley of very stately horse-chestnut trees with their glory of white-and-rose blossoms in the young summer like heavenly candles. This alley opened upon a golden graveled rondel in front of the entrance to the house.

At the rear, behind hedges of lilac bushes, were the many doors which led to the various compartments of this busy castle. And it was mostly behind those back doors that we lived our daily life, very comradely, intermingled with the staff of employees and servants that not only were a part of the household, but also our inherited trusted friends. After all, our lives were theirs and it was really they who completed with their simple, practical wisdom the rigid educational system of our youth. And so quite naturally we learned about flowers and trees and fruits—about herbs which grew in long rows back of the kitchen quarters and close to the *potager.* We adored herbs because they came early in the spring with their unassuming beauty and their generous fragrance. Bouquets of herbs dried slowly in garnet vases in our schoolroom.

Many a time I have seen my own grandmother step out from her summer pavilion in the early morning hours, a very lithe and graceful figure in her changeable taffeta dress, lace fichu and a little parasol in her hands. Courageously she walked in her heelless light slippers first through the damp earthen rows of her flower gardens; then she would turn and cross a lawn to the herb gardens. I have seen her kneel down almost to caress some small bushes, and I knew that they were her tarragons which she watched closely because they had such a hard time acclimatizing themselves, having been brought from the south of Russia. The tarragon had remained a sickly struggling plant until a barrel of soil had been brought to my grandmother by one of those traveling Tartar merchants. They came to our castle every two years with all the strange wonders of the oriental and warm world to which they belonged. The arrival of our Tartar was most spectacular. It was like a show when he entered the great gate, sitting erect on a beautiful black horse, his silver-embroidered tunic reaching to his soft leather boots, and around his head a many-colored turban. Behind him were his two servants who carried his wares on pack-mules.

Grandmother received her Tartar most enthusiastically, with a great reverence and a strange etiquette. After the bowing ceremonies were over the Tartar waved his hand in a grandiose manner and his two young "tartarides" jumped forward noiselessly, placed the rolls and boxes on the floor, and swiftly unrolled and opened them. Dear grandmother had two rosy spots on her soft cheeks. It was all too wonderful with the unpacking of the silks, velvets, brocades, perfumes, spices, and seeds —seeds for herbs to grow!

Years after, when I was growing up, the Tartar merchants came by train, most prosaically—and third class, too—and finally Tartars never came again. This colorful event was no more. All our precious seeds and oils were sent us from London. Then grandmother, incredibly old and more incredibly young, often told me that the visits of her Tartar had been wonderful interludes in her life and a real enlightenment. Grandmother certainly was an authority on herbs and plants, and even now when I read of new medical discoveries which are derived from Nature's fabulous treasure-house I think of grandmother's laboratory and pharmacy with reverence.

We shared and enjoyed all those herb adventures tremendously, but to completely understand them one would have had to live in this atmosphere where herbs and the right use of herbs were a sacred tradition. When still children we were permitted to take an active part in the harvesting of herbs in the gardens and in the fields and woods. We learned about the wild-growing herbs around which fairy tales and witchcraft were woven; herbs which had passionate-looking flowers; some which held the secret of life and death within their leaves and roots. These herbs we and the village children were strictly forbidden ever to touch.

Yes, happily we romped with all these children—

holidays for us without the surveillance of governesses; we picked leaves, herbs, and berries, and proudly delivered our baskets at the herb house into the hands of the peasant women who were the herb-house keepers and who by instinct and heredity knew all about herbs and what to do with them.

Food and herbs were inseparable to us; automatically we associated them in our daily menus. To me it was indeed a phenomenon to discover that a cook could do without these delicate seasonings. Their use was not a luxury only for the nobleman's table; they belonged just as much, and even more, to the humblest of people. It was really the peasants who firmly established and placed herbs where they belong; it was they who first found the extraordinary combinations of herbs for dishes which became "national dishes" and survived all historical calamities. And by their national dishes one easily can discover the characteristics of a people—strong or fiery, sleepy or resigned.

Undoubtedly it was the shepherds who discovered interesting concoctions of meats, herbs and wild vegetables. At sundown and in the restfulness of the slowly approaching night, these lonely men would sit by the tripod overhanging a charcoal fire on which a wonderful mixture had been simmering for hours. And in the mountains the wild hunters and woodcutters, probably craving and searching for greens, discovered the wonders of wild herbs and berries, mushrooms, and the wild garlic which made their barbecue a noble food. They used everything edible they could find, pine needles included. All these mixtures marinated and permeated the meat and eventually brought about a civilized modification which, after all, distinguished their dish as a meal in contrast with their former carnivorous feeding.

When I was seventeen, a very young seventeen, I discovered the diary of my ancestor. This came about as the consequence of a romantic curiosity. That looks strange written down in cold letters, yet it was just that. Her portrait hung, the last of a row, in the long hall, young and beautiful among all the elderly men and women. This portrait of our ancestor had haunted me. My heart always beat a little faster looking at her. She was so strangely alive—her half-closed eyes following me sometimes sadly and very often mockingly.

Her name was Sophie Anasthasia, and all that we children knew was that she came from Greek ancestors who had fled before the Turks in the fifteenth century and landed in the Carpathians. Great-grandmother Sophie had died young, and it was this aureole that made her so outstanding in a gallery of older women and men.

I broke a sacred tradition when I began to pry into Sophie Anasthasia's personal history which, with so many others, was locked away in records kept in beautiful old chests in the attic of our castle. An attic filled with old chests and memories of many centuries would mean in some houses a cobwebby, spooky, ghost-haunted place where bats made their headquarters. But this attic of ours was kept as the most solemn, sun-flooded memorial hall where visitors would only whisper and walk on tiptoes.

With fiercely trembling fingers I turned the heavy bronze key in the chest on which great-grandmother's name was engraved. I sat quite still in front of the open chest, my heart beating in my temples. I looked at the many pigeon-holes inside the beautifully carved lid and it was there that I discovered the strange, sentimental-looking book. The cover was embroidered in the finest *petit-point,* with a wreath of seed pearls around a heart pierced by an arrow. On the first page it read in hand-painted letters, "My Diary."

I hurriedly locked the chest and with the book pressed against my heart I tiptoed silently out of the attic and sped down the many stairs. I arrived in my room in a state of nervous exhaustion, as if I had done something very wicked. I wrapped myself in a cashmere shawl, crouching down in one of the big *fauteuils,* and felt better in its safe protection. I untied the silken ribbons which held together the fine leaves of the book covered with the pale handwriting of Sophie Anasthasia.

I turned page after page; I sat for hours—I sat until the sun faded and twilight filled the room, tired and almost crushed by a disappointment which shook the exalted expectations of my young soul.

The diary of Sophie Anasthasia seemed no more than the recording of daily occurrences laconically told, without even emphasizing the birth of her two sons and her only daughter. Wars, pestilence, and human misery were sketched with a few poignant words—impersonal and detached—but what was inconceivable and inexplicable to me was that every day's record invariably closed on menus, newly discovered recipes, or on a formula for beauty preparations, and on new patterns of *petit-point* and frivolity laces. I was greatly confused.

For days I was upset in my mind. But while turning those pale pages, again and again, the extraordinary thing happened that her menus, her banquets, her recipes even, became fascinating reading to me. There were, I saw, little witty observations about her guests, carefully draped over with conventional words. Sometimes it was as if she jested with menus and sumptuous preparations for those banquets—enormous eating feasts which must have lasted for hours. Most daringly she had them interrupted, between courses, by fencing matches, or by minuets, or by charades—while lackeys were circulating with cooling *tisanes* and sobering almond milk. Finally with a mischievous command, "*Changez les dames*," she had her guests returned to the tables.

It suddenly became absolutely clear to me that there was a deeper meaning, a definitite purpose, in this diary which was not comprehensible to me. I needed help badly and I needed help from Marushka. Marushka! Even now when all these happenings have become memories to me, the thought of Marushka still fills me with a deep nostalgia for all that Marushka has been for me. This living soul of kindness and dramatic simplicity, was the genius, the fairy who reigned supreme over the grandiose kitchen of our castle, our big chef—and she was a peasant woman. She cannot be separated from the kitchen of my home. It was like a whole world, this kitchen—sunbeams streaming through long, high windows that made all the copper kettles from the biggest to the tiniest on the long wall gleam as if there were life and blood in metal.

The afternoon hours were Marushka's own. It was very still in the kitchen when I slid across the velvety red brick floor. And to her I sobbed out my disenchantment and my dilemma. Marushka listened gravely, holding all the time the beautiful book in her hands, stroking it tenderly and with great reverence. She asked me to read from the book to her. Her big quiet eyes shone with tears. "Oh, the great book," she whispered. Marushka turned to me suddenly as if some decision were made up in her mind. "Leonka," she said, "will you leave this noble book with me for one day?"

I left it with Marushka, and later I knew that she had told my father all about it and he had consented to let us have Sophie Anasthasia's diary.

Both of us, Marushka and I, became fanatically absorbed in this diary. It was Marushka with her simple primitive soul and her naïve intuition who could read between words and lines, could read of Sophie Anasthasia's joys, disillusions, and finally her own defeat. The diary closed abruptly after her thirty-fourth birthday. Though crowded with an overwhelming knowledge of the cuisine—of all the thousand details of which modern cooking has no actual need—with all of this my ancestor's diary never could have been called a cookbook. It was something much more—it was a deep study; it was imagination and reality and it was great poetry.

My father had been impressed by our work of bringing Sophie Anasthasia's strange diary to life and he had it printed in illuminated letters and sent to a culinary exhibition in Vienna. Back came for me a little golden medal which very proudly I carried around my neck on a velvet ribbon for years. But I insisted that Marushka should wear it on great holidays, and when I married into far Russia, I left the little medal with her.

Now we have the modern kitchen, the modern life, and we have to harmonize the daily menus with our modern tempo. More and more has to be deducted from the opulence of the food of yesterday. We have to conform to a stream-lined style—not alone in clothes. Leaves taken from the diary of my ancestor, ideas exciting and amusing from all my years of travel will help to extract a sober fineness from an *embarras de richesse*. Especially do I want this book to become a guide to lead many into a new adventure—cooking with herbs. I am certain in my heart, after consulting spiritually my ancestor Sophie Anasthasia, that she would get a tremendous thrill out of thc fact of having her *esprit de cuisine* translated and handed down to the Americans—to a land which during her lifetime had been a vision of something for which people then already longed.

CHAPTER TWO

The Fine Herbs and the Robust Herbs

WHAT WE READ ABOUT HERBS—and there is quite a number of fascinating new herb books on the market—has somewhat amazed those who were raised on herbs and who consider the addition of herbs to the *cuisine* as much a matter of course as others consider the use of salt and pepper.

This revival is most interesting, yet it is still too complicated in its pretentious appearance to make cooking with herbs quite as popular and generally accepted as it really deserves. What I wish to achieve with this book is to let everyone in on the herb mysteries—and let them in, in the easiest way. Herbs are so small, so unassuming, so belonging to the surroundings of pots and pans, that it is unfair not to make room for their fragrance on the kitchen shelf.

I would like to be able to show everyone an herb farm, such as the one on the outskirts of Washington, where I now live. I really don't like the word "farm" for something that is so exquisite, and which has grown purely from the ingenuity, the profound knowledge, of one great woman whose memory I have the desire to honor. This farm is an herb garden so charming, so everything that herbs are and mean, that it is outright perfection. It is all there—the mystery of the past, of the ancients, in the herb house built from century-old wood, in the solemn quiet of the shadowy beam-ceilinged room with the huge fireplace, with old emblems and books around, with sprays of fragrancies hanging from rafters—everything from old witchcraft and primitive brewing utensils to modern facilities. The air is filled with the cozy scents of old-fashioned *potpourri* and sweet lavender in open baskets and quaint bowls. What a room! What a symbol and what an atmosphere amazingly created with the live beauty of an almost overwhelming abundance of colorful flowers.

People are making pilgrimage to this house, to these gardens, curious and bewildered. They walk about, not quite comprehending why, behind protecting boxwood, all the rows of little bushy and stretching plants are growing, and what it is all about. They stand puzzled in front of the neatly labeled jars on old shelves, mostly Greek to them, until their faces light up when they discover that sage belongs to all these mysteries too—sage which goes in the turkey and which everybody knows!

Still they walk about the gardens and they are strangely attracted and affected because they would like to know more.

Shall this be a new cookbook about herbs? With all the wealth of cookbooks in this country! Or one of herb recipes? Strangely, there is not such a thing as an herb recipe. Herbs are nothing more than an *addition,* but a much needed one, to the millions of recipes now in existence and doing without them. Yet after all, how are herbs to be made known, and by what practical methods should herbs be used in cooking? Practical methods? Here again I am somewhat stumbling because herbs are really a most undisciplined, free-lancing lot—herbs are a touch, an accent, a great charm to foods, a kind of refining novelty. Also they are remedies homeopathically dispensed, yet constantly helping to tone up the digestion and purify the precious blood in our veins. Yes, they are all of that, and herbs are not a new invention, herbs are gloriously old, sacred and reverential. There is the same profound meaning in the word "herb" as in the word "bread"! Bread, the staff of life, bread from the earth, and herbs, the masterful little healers, grown from the earth! Each little herb stores in its seed, leaf, or root, an oil which not only gives refreshing delicate flavors to our foods but has a mysterious refreshing influence upon our days. And this is not a fairy tale or old-fashioned superstition; it is one of the eternal truths of nature which has been disregarded or forgotten. And now suddenly herbs are to come to life again in this country, bashfully, but they are here!

For the clear understanding of herbs used in cooking, I believe it is necessary to divide the culinary herbs into two distinctive groups:

A. The Fine Herbs
B. The Robust Herbs

THE FINE HERBS

Sweet Basil	Rosemary
Chervil	Tarragon
Sweet Marjoram	Chive (?)
French or Garden Thyme	

It was undoubtedly the French who established this group as superior to the group B herbs and it is they who are responsible for the name: *Les Fines Herbes* which means, of course, the fine herbs. The fine herbs are the domineering ones in flavor, and a long tradition connects them with certain dishes, either as a group or a part of the group, and also individually. This however does not mean that everybody who uses herbs in cooking is bound to one hereditary order or to the advice which great chefs have left behind. It is one of the alluring qualities of herbs that they cannot be tied to rules. Neither should the fine herbs as a whole group be used altogether; this certainly would be too overwhelming in aroma and not quite congenial. For this reason the group divides itself by affinities and characteristics into three small groups, and even then it is the cook who in the end will decide the right combination.

From experience the following three small groups blend perfectly:

1.	2.	3.
Sweet Basil	Sweet Marjoram	Rosemary
Chervil	Garden Thyme	Tarragon

In the list which I have called "The Fine Herbs," chive is placed with a question mark. Chive decidedly belongs to the onion family and by heritage does not belong to this exclusive circle of herbs. Yet in the final analysis of the fine herbs, single or in groups, the association of chive with the fine herbs will justify itself.

These six herbs of group A are definitely most individual in their flavor and effect, and the selection is entirely up to the cook who knows the likes, dislikes, the psychology, or idiosyncrasies of the persons for whom she or he cooks. When the fine herbs are used individually they often have to be toned down because their fragrance is too outstanding to rely on one individual herb for flavor. Again, this leads to very interesting experiments which will delight the intelligent cook, and often will lead her into the camp of the robust herbs which for their substantialness are good to draw on.

I am explaining all this as a defense measure because I am desirous that this book shall become a help and a guide. It might be regarded as a fashion plate which for the individual taste has to be modified or enhanced. The cook has complete freedom to use her or his own tested recipes—the addition of the right combination of herbs will probably freshen up old, brave recipes which suddenly will find themselves in line with the latest style in foods.

But first of all the cook must become herb-conscious. What is the meaning of being herb-conscious? Can this be explained? It has something to do with the senses, as has the use of perfumes, which is so very often misunderstood. If people are fragrance-conscious they will avoid, in choice and quantity, perfume which is obnoxious to the ordinarily sensitive nose.

To become herb-conscious means to study the individual aromas of the herbs, to learn to distinguish them, to love them, and to use them. Experiment! Try all kinds of mixtures, try a dash of this, of that, and in the end individually preferred combinations are discovered. It is great fun.

SWEET BASIL

Sweet basil is the one among the strong clan of basils which is used in cooking. The royal basil, the overwhelming, glorious one, is a wonderfully decorative plant. Its aroma is pompous and its leaves are used most effectively as a finishing touch to green salad. But it is the green curly-leaved sweet basil which has the rich herb quality. This makes basil a wonderful standby to enliven the more insipid-tasting vegetables. It is decidedly a valuable part of one of the groups which are designated as salad herbs; individually it is used in basil butter for sandwiches, is delicious with egg dishes and added to broiled tomatoes and onions. It is as stimulating as a fine liqueur.

CHERVIL

Chervil is the noble cousin of the parsleys. The flavor of chervil is so tender that it should be used more generously than other herbs. Chervil needs the support of other herbs badly. In the first group we tie basil to chervil and this is a very good combination. But strange as it seems, it is there too that the humble chive is the happy medium which makes this combination perfect. In the group of salad herbs chervil prefers to be tied to one of the more robust herbs of which we will learn further on. Individually, chervil can be highly recommended for use in soups, especially in green "spring soups"; also in egg dishes, in green sauces for fresh-water fish, or sprinkled, finely cut, over potato or celery-root salad, or in a dressing for the hearts of artichokes.

SWEET MARJORAM

Sweet marjoram is the great marshal of the herbs—an entity in itself. It is a most amiable herb, a favorite of cooks. But such good things have their bad points too. The aroma of sweet marjoram has to be somewhat subdued, otherwise it is all over the place. Marjoram should be in the company of thyme, which also is strong in its characteristics, but of a sterner character. Yet if I can get hold of a sprig of fresh marjoram I sense the delight I used to have in the famous potato soup of our home. It is a delicious addition to scalloped potatoes, or to turnips and cole slaw, or in a green sauce for broccoli. Green peas have a *penchant* for sweet marjoram. Also it is the most popular herb for modifying heavy meats, as: pork, duck, mutton, and also turkeys. Yes, turkey! And without dethroning forever good old sage, the cook should venture to try sweet marjoram in the dressing. That will draw some ahs! and ohs! on Thanksgiving Day.

ROSEMARY

Rosemary is an herb of biblical legend; it is a wonder shrub, slender, a dignified soft green, stretching itself above the average herbs. The fragrance of its fine needle-like leaves reminds one of incense. It is amazing that rosemary really condescended to be called a culinary herb, even though ranged among the finest ones. It was the herb with which the church was decorated on great holidays and for weddings, and its essence was often used instead of the oriental myrrh. But the Latin people love holy things to enter their daily life, and they have changed rosemary into a worldly herb by associating it with thyme and a whiff of chive. And really it is delicious and very unusual in poultry dressing or in a marinade for spring or baby lamb—their Easter offering. In Florence, fennel or *finocchio* when braised will have rosemary in its juices; and once I discovered a faint touch of rosemary in the French *bouillabaisse,* the grim saffron in this fish having a hard time being subdued by the holy rosemary.

TARRAGON

Tarragon is forever the most festive herb and the delight of gourmets. Tarragon is the one herb that can stand on its own entirely. At home, when tarragon was brought to us from the south of Russia, and solemnly planted on our soil, it was our *enfant gâté* and was called *esdragon.* Later I found among French peasants the legend of *esdragon,* which meant *l'herbe au dragon,* and it was known as a medicinal herb to heal bites of mad dogs. And *estragon* it was all over the world with the exception of this country; for, when I went in search of *estragon* here, there was not such an herb to be known in the United States of America. When finally I discovered it in New York it was at one of the polyglot Eastside markets, at the greenstand of a fat Italian who had strewn it nonchalantly among the salads and vegetables. I was overjoyed. "*Estragon,*" I exclaimed. The Italian pointed his first finger into my face. "Tarragon, *signora,* I raised it myself." And tarragon it is now for me, tarragon with its spear-like leaves, velvety green and its exquisite fragrance. Tarragon can walk in on any dish and, whenever it is there, right away it becomes an unusual dish. But strangely, tarragon in the minds of most people is connected with tarragon vinegar. True, tarragon vinegar is a very rare thing because it takes an abundance of tarragon not to be killed by the strong vinegar's individuality. The French cultivate it in great quantity especially for this purpose and submerge the fresh tarragon herbs in the finest unadulterated wine vinegar.

FRENCH OR GARDEN THYME

Garden thyme is of great intensity and also is capable of standing its ground individually. In the various groups of herbs it is not the thyme that is looking for support but the other herbs which want to be in the company of thyme. Thyme might be called a pedigreed herb, for it was first discovered near Athens on the classic Mount Hymettus. Whoever has been in Greece has been served with honey from Mount Hymettus, made by the bees of Athens who feasted on thyme. Thyme is an all-around herb for the *cuisine* either individually or in a group. It will never spoil the fun—has the quality of a splendid mixer. Thyme is also a great medium in the world of perfumes and has very valuable medicinal qualities. In Switzerland, thyme is always used with its medicinal powers in mind. Thyme as *tisane* brings happy dreams, and in the Alps one is served with a goat cheese permeated with wild thyme. Fortunately it is the thyme that overpowers the goat. The uses of thyme are legion and the cook who knows herbs will never be without thyme.

CHIVE

And here is chive finishing the group of the fine herbs. Indeed, chive has wormed itself into the inner circle of this exclusive *milieu* of fine herbs to stay as the one indispensable herb. Chive, the *trait d'union,* the liaison herb, the medium that brings all the herb flavors under one flag! It will improve, it will tone down, it will heighten, and for the cook it will always do the last trick. When the soup is somewhat insipid or the sauce colorless, a dash of chive will enliven the soup and will make the sauce hopeful looking. In chive there is the element of the onion qualities but refined and non-belligerent. Chive is the cook's best friend, and there should never be a kitchen window sill without a large pot of chive. If summer comes and chive grows in the garden, it develops to a most decorative plant with its canopy of blue flowers.

Herbs altogether have a short-lived season. When at their best they have to be cut in midsummer and placed in the herb house to dry; and to be further used, crushed or powdered, packed in neat jars, closed tightly and labeled. If herbs are let alone, they only go to seed without leaving any trace of their wonderful qualities even when dried. If cut in time and dried they lose little of their fragrance; then as soon as they are warmed up in butter or oil they begin to fill the kitchen with the happy aroma of herb bouquet.

The experience of our mothers and grandmothers and of a great many herbalists—tradition and formula left behind—tell of very useful and happy combinations of herbs. There are excellent omelet herbs (combined) used in the famous French *omelette aux fines herbes, ragoût* herbs for sauces, and herbs for salad dressing. Still the doors are wide open for the cook to change all these combinations and to try the salad herbs in the omelet and vice versa. When dry herbs are used in the *cuisine* it is again chive which gives the illusion of fresh herbs—because chive is never dried. There is also the other indispensable herb colleague of the robust herbs, parsley, which often saves the day if the greenness of the dish is at stake.

Yet one should know the quantity of herbs to be used

in the dried stage, compared with the quantity used of green herbs. If the recipes *indicate a tablespoon of fresh herbs chopped or cut, half a teaspoon of dried herbs would be the equivalent and one-fourth of a teaspoon when the herbs are powdered.*

The real lovers of herbs will insist upon, first: raising their own herbs—a minimum of six different kinds if the space is very small. To have the joy of cutting one's own fresh herbs in winter, I recommend—if there is a southwest window available—planting at least the fine herbs in a box, not only for the great joy of cutting them fresh daily, but for the beauty and fragrance of such a box. The plants will expand in the warmth of the room and fill the house with the noble aromas which nature implanted in these little herbs.

THE ROBUST HERBS

This selection is made from experience and practical use. The need of these robust herbs is concrete, not imaginary and for the perfume only. There is no extravagance of taste or foreign fad included. Some of the herbs listed below belong on the kitchen shelves. They always should be there, just like salt and pepper.

Borage	Winter Savory
Wild Marjoram (*Origanum vulgare*)	Sorrel
	Caraway
Pot Marjoram	Fennel
Mint	Dill
Sage	Horseradish
Summer Savory	Parsley

These herbs are a daily standby to make the *cuisine* palatable and variegated. There are no rules whatsoever—just learn to know their individual value in the seasoning for the daily meals. It is absolutely a matter of taste and not of a definite plan; therefore I shall tell only of experiences which might be either followed or changed.

The revival of herbs has something to do with the modern trend of living in America. The universal taste for foods has become more precise, more definite, as the great variety of dishes has narrowed down to the essential. But alas, the essential has become very monotonous. In far too many homes and restaurants the four kinds of meats—beef, lamb, veal, and pork—make the round always in the same identical uniform. There are no surprises. Yet there could be most agreeable surprises, using the robust herbs. These greatly help heavy meats—they modify, and they make heroic flavors.

The robust herbs, too, are anxious to be introduced individually, because they are the hardier ones and very seldom demand support or company. But they do not object if the fine herbs approach the robust ones for their solid background.

BORAGE

Borage, first of all, is beautiful to look at; its foliage is rough, but of a roughness like rough velvet and of the same softness of sheen. Its green is softly shaded and its flowers are wonderfully blue. A sprig of borage in the pot with cooking cauliflower, or cooked with lentils, or used with braised beef or *ragoût* is a decisive improvement. Yet it does not dominate. And borage placed in tea or light white wine makes a delicious cooling drink in summertime.

WILD MARJORAM

I am most partial to wild marjoram. It has an undefinable charm. It is indispensable for the Latin cook and in the Orient. *Origanum,* as it is also called, in the marinade for lamb and fowl, or in the stuffing of meats, immediately brings out new flavors. Wild marjoram is not often used but it can be purchased at all Italian or Spanish shops.

POT MARJORAM

Pot marjoram is a very solid herb and very influential in heavy meats and meat dishes. It doesn't need the tender treatment of the fine herbs, which never should be submitted to much cooking. The fine herbs are the last touch in the *cuisine* while the robust herbs cook with the food from start to finish, and therefore have a voice in the dish itself.

MINT

Mint is the darling of the kitchen. And such a utility herb! Yet mint really should belong to the fine herbs because mint is a touch to be added when the food is ready for serving.

SAGE

Sage, the ever-ready one, should be used most carefully because its strong aromatic and spicy qualities bear down on foods and it is difficult to subdue it. It is parsley only which will mellow the character of sage somewhat if mixed generously with it.

SUMMER SAVORY

Summer savory is little known and yet so universally exquisite. It adds flavor to pale vegetables and moderates hearty vegetables such as the cabbages, Brussels sprouts, turnips, and dried peas and beans. Summer savory influences the odors of the cabbages when cooking. It is a delicious addition to potato soups and boiled with ham or any kind of boiled meats.

WINTER SAVORY

Winter savory, truly a very useful herb, belongs to pots and pans. It also is an interesting herb, quite surprising in salad dressing, for potato salad or Russian salad, or in fish stews, or combined with vegetables in steamed fish. It is fun to experiment with the savories. I only recently discovered how excellent winter savory is in egg dishes and cold sauces.

SORREL

Sorrel is an herb and a most exquisite vegetable all in one. It is badly neglected in this country. In the Viennese and French *cuisines* it is used daily one way or another, for flavoring and looks. First because of its tender greenness, and then for the lemon-like tang. It is so deliciously tart for soup, chilled or hot, salad, or green vegetable.

HORSERADISH

Horseradish is a root but ranks among the robust herbs. It is the finest among all condiments if not mistreated and misunderstood. Horseradish has been the victim of the ever-ready era and erroneously has been placed on the same level and conserved in the same way as mustard. But horseradish is a root and not a powder. Horseradish has to be freshly grated only as needed. It sympathizes with lemon juice, and lemon juice (unlike vinegar) preserves the horseradish flavor. As a condiment, as a sauce, or in its natural state—simply grated to be served with meats or fish—it is easily digestible and a great appetizer.

DILL

Pickling made dill famous. It is a most beautiful growing plant of a sourly penetrating aroma when in the green state. And it is a surprising herb. There is no other herb which gives fish dishes such glamour. Its greenness is fascinating and the fine fern-like sprigs and leaves are very decorative. Sandwiches made with dill butter are most unusual. Of course it is only a summer dish. (There is never dried dill in the little jar.) There are dill seeds also, which are used in the pickling.

FENNEL

Fennel is the most classic of herbs and an eternal one. It is used in the kitchen, in the nursery, and in pharmacies for the benefit of mankind—but there is the Florence fennel, or *finocchio*, a live root which is a glorious appetizer when eaten raw (instead of celery) and a noble dish when braised and served with Parmesan cheese. The stems of growing fennel make a very tender vegetable for cooking.

CARAWAY

Caraway seed is a momentum for the *cuisine*. I know that I never could do without caraway seed. It is at the bottom of the flavor of many dishes and it always has the last word. When using all kinds of vegetable stock for soup, one learns that caraway seed has the strong quality of bones and meats together and at the same time the refreshing body of a plant alive. It also stimulates the digestion of certain "heavy" foods. Fennel tea and caraway tea are the standbys in the nursery for baby—and despite all the newest inventions for relieving gas, the nurse finally turns to the old remedies to make the infant comfortable.

The laboratories have wide use for caraway and fennel seeds in medicinal formulas; and for anise which has the same quality but is very little used nowadays unless it has become a part of the combined dry spices such as curry powder, and the many other mixtures concocted in the Orient where people adore pungent aromas. Caraway, anise, and fennel are the underlying flavors for many liqueur concoctions.

PARSLEY

And greatest of all robust herbs is parsley. When the old herbs were disregarded by the people in this country, they held on to parsley—little enough, using it mostly as garnish to have their dishes look appetizing. And what would the cooking world be without parsley? Pages could be written about its uses, not as a simple garnishing but as the most serious factor for the betterment of almost all soups, cold and hot sauces, and as the basic herb for the marinades of fishes and meats. A kitchen without parsley is surely devoid of the best, the most essential flavoring, the most modest one—and a flavoring of which one never tires. It never pushes itself to the foreground but always is the humble partner for one or another of the fine herbs. And finally, parsley has been of great medicinal value since time immemorial.

CHAPTER THREE

Herbs, Spices, and Berries

THERE IS A STRONG CORRELATION between herbs and spices. Spices are often classed with herbs, and so are some berries. Yet herbs are a diffident kind of plant, herbs are haughty; spices are expected to coördinate themselves with herbs. This again is a problem, because spices are outstanding in their characteristics, which are stronger than those of the herbs. Yet if both are rightly coupled they blend exquisitely. Certain berries become spices when ground. (The peppers.) Juniper berries bring the aroma of the woods, and are indispensable when it comes to the marinading of meats from the woods—yet they are just as interesting in the marinades for tame meats. Juniper berries are used with great success in curing ham.

The reputation of spices goes way back to the ancient Phœnicians who crossed the seven seas to exchange their spices, which were roots and barks and berries, and were worth their weight in gold. But since the spices are no longer gained at the point of the dagger or for the outlay of gold, but are shelved prosaically in grocery stores, they are treated casually—their romantic past forgotten. Herbs have had a different career. They have kept a certain mystifying influence upon mankind, and now that herbs—with a newly polished halo—have come to the foreground again, spices are profiting by this association and have resumed a more important standing. Where there are herbs on the kitchen shelves there must be spices to complete a campaign for reviving noble seasonings which are grown from nature for the glory of the *cuisine.*

Many spices used discreetly in food help the digestion.

SPICES USED IN COMBINATION WITH HERBS

Curry powder (a mixture)	Pepperoni	Saffron
Bay leaves	Paprika	Coriander
Cumin	Cinnamon	Cardamon
Ginger	Vanilla	Cloves
The peppers	Nutmeg	Mustard powder
(black, white, and red)	Mace	

Thanks to modern progress curry powder and other ready-ground and mixed spices may be bought ready for use. In years gone by these preparations had to be individually ground and mixed by cooks. Nevertheless it is not just a fad to grate pepper berries freshly when needed instead of using the ready-mixed powder. Indeed the freshly grated pepper has the whole rich aroma of the berry. And fortunately the little French pepper mills are seen more and more on American dinner tables today. To grind your pepper as needed is now not only clever but popular.

The curry powders (combinations of several spices) which are on the market are on the whole excellently blended and so are the mixed ground spices which are the interesting spice *potpourri*. The flavors of some spices alone are too arrogant for certain uses but in an ensemble they are most agreeable. Yet it is necessary for the intelligent cook to know of what the various combinations consist.

From the leaves of my ancestor's old book I possess a very interesting formula for curry powder. It must be first-hand because it came as a great novelty then from one of the fantastic Tartar merchants who roamed the world and brought some of its wonders to my grandmother's door.

CURRY POWDER

It is not necessary to give the exact measurements of the spices used, for no one today will attempt to grind these berries, barks, nuts, and seeds. The combination used is:

Yellow ginger (*Curcuma*)	Caraway seed	Cinnamon stick
	Mustard seed	Red pepper
Black pepper	Cumin	

From the ancestral diary, too, comes another interesting combination of spices which can be used for *ragoûts*:

Thyme, 1 tablespoon (if freshly cut)
1 teaspoon (if dried)
Bay leaves, 2 leaves finely cut
Shallots, 1 tablespoon grated
Garlic, 1 clove grated
Black pepper, 1½ teaspoons grated
Mixed spices, ¼ teaspoon powdered
Nutmeg, ¼ teaspoon powdered
Ginger, ¼ teaspoon powdered.

This mixture keeps well in an air-tight tin box. It is important that the cook should be aware of the ingredients of powders and condiments which are freely used. Some play havoc with a sensitive digestion. In any case all exotic seasoning should be sparingly used.

CUMIN

Cumin is a seed plant like caraway, fennel, and anise, often mentioned in the category of herbs. Yet cumin decidedly should be classed as a spice because the seeds only are used. Cumin always has been used most carefully and sparingly. Its pungency reeks through everything which is tender and aromatic, and yet if a few seeds of cumin are added to a benevolent spice mixture it immediately becomes an interesting combination. It is used in curry powder too, and it is unmistakable that cumin *is* in the mixture. Cumin is a part of many Spanish, Mexican, and Italian dishes—it is less popular in Central Europe. A few seeds with the well-known *arroz con pollo* give great piquancy to the dish, or a few seeds in the rice which is baked in the oven oriental style are intriguing. Cumin has its place in the *cuisine* too, but it is a spice to be studied and used with discretion.

GINGER

Ginger belongs to the herb family, although it also ranges with the spices. This is a great favorite of mine;

it has the fine flexible pungency which goes with heavy sauces or marinades; it also fits into cakes; it is a great adjuster for an upset digestion.

THE PEPPERS

The black and white peppers differ only as far as the color is concerned; they both have the same effect in seasoning, the black one a trifle stronger. Although pepper is an inoffensive spice it is advisable to go easy with it. There are two forms of East Indian pepper which have a specially green, aromatic taste—the black is called Tellicherry, the white, Sarawak. They are imported and can be procured at any fine grocery store. *Cayenne* is the red, the most vicious pepper, yet the most interesting one. Of cayenne never more than a *soupçon,* a thought more than a deed. And in spite of this reputation, strangely enough, an atom of red pepper has an instantaneous soothing influence upon a rebellious stomach.

PEPPERONI

Pepperoni is a rival of cayenne, more difficult to use because it is treacherous; and it is good to know that its use should be kept to an amount somewhere below a dash. There is a great distance between the green and red peppers of our familiar daily use and the pepperoni. They too are vicious members of the pepper family. Nevertheless the Spanish, Mexican, and Italian people would never cook without them.

PAPRIKA

On the contrary, the mild offspring of those pompous pepperonis, paprika, has great individuality and its use has no bad effect. Paprika gives a warm taste and color to sauces and gravies. This is the Balkans' great national spice. In fact it has had a certain influence on the temperament of the people along the Danube—fiery and amiable they are and they don't need a stimulant such as alcohol to lift them to high exhilaration. It really is their food which gives an exquisite stimulant.

CINNAMON

Cinnamon is the inner bark of a laurel tree. Such unbelievable goodness, so aromatic and so unadulterated! In dark sauces for duck and game it gives a mysterious touch, not to mention the many other pleasant qualities cinnamon possesses. In cake and buns, on toasts—and what a delicious topping for the pale puddings, like blank sheets of paper until the interesting color of cinnamon is written or painted upon them. The pudding, when cinnamon's warm brown color floods it, suddenly becomes a delicious dish. Cinnamon is a wonderful spice!

VANILLA

Vanilla, strictly speaking, is not a spice. Plagiarism has been committed in the name of vanilla; for the little vanilla bean, the fruit of a beautifully graceful orchid-like flower of heavenly fragrance, should be used fresh for good effect, not simply as a faint flavor in some chemical "extract." And if once you have tried this little bean as a bean, expanding its aroma in hot cream or wine, or placed in your tightly covered sugar canister, to be used for mixing in cake, it will be unforgettable.

NUTMEG AND MACE

Nutmeg and mace derive from the same plant. Nutmeg is a very individual spice and it must be remembered that nutmeg is exceedingly prominent when and wherever it is used. Therefore go easy on flavoring with nutmeg. It is very useful as a combination spice. Alone it never lets the cook down, yet there are some who are not over-enthusiastic about eating cake, custard, or a sauce whose own flavor is entirely obliterated by nutmeg.

SAFFRON

The genuine, the East Indian, saffron is the most expensive of all spices. When saffron was brought to my great-grandmother Sophie it was not meant to be used as a spice. It was a wonderful dyestuff—warm and golden yellow with green lights in it. And since saffron was a flower (or, as the chemist would classify it, a vegetable dye), the plant not poisonous, my ancestor did not hesitate to dip a few threads of saffron fabric in the bouillon. The soup accepted not only the beautiful color, but it also changed the taste, acquiring a strange, exotic flavor which we found very agreeable. And probably the same thing which was tried by my great-grandmother was tried by other ancestors in Spain, Italy, and France, and by all the chefs and *cordons bleus* everywhere in Europe. And what would the famous French *bouillabaisse* be without saffron? This is an interesting addition to many a *ragoût fin* or to certain rice dishes. It is a rare spice and worth some study.

CORIANDER AND CARDAMON

While the coriander plant has a most disagreeable odor the seed is very aromatic and is a helpful addition to combinations of spices. Cardamon seed is individual and widely used in many cake recipes as well as with meats and game. (The Southern belles chewed cardamon a great deal as a breath sweetener.)

CLOVES

The clove is a lovable spice, reminding one of carnations in its aroma. It is dominant in the allspice mixture which is used in *ragoûts,* soups, sauces and stuffings, rounding out the combination of the strong accents of black pepper, mustard seed, bay leaves, and pimiento. It is used especially in this country to tone down the penetrating flavor of the ham crust. Ground cloves are very useful—just a whiff will give a brown sauce the final touch.

MUSTARD

Mustard is one of the eternal spices—it is widely known and used. One mustard plant produces the dark seed and another has a white seed, actually a lemon-colored seed. The black one when ground is used in the famous condiment, French mustard, whilst the other is what is known as English mustard. The uses of powdered English mustard are not explored as far as they might be. If rightly understood this seed is one of great utility, and might save the day for many a sauce which otherwise is hopelessly colorless in taste and appearance.

CHAPTER FOUR

Exploring Herbs in Cooking

HERBS SHOULD BE INTRODUCED GRADUALLY to a family which has never used herbs—yes, casually and unobtrusively—indeed they must remain the veiled mystery of the menu. The improvement of certain dishes soon will be noticed, and then the veil can be lifted.

Families are apt to refuse innovations, to criticize or ridicule them. I have seen this happen because at first the cook was too generous with her herbal offerings. Immediately there was a storm let loose around the dinner table—outright revolt. "What did you do to the gravy? Put some coughdrops in it?" or "Is there any of us you would like to poison?" Yet perseveringly she went on—getting wiser—and in the end the young husband of the house helped his wife plant an herb garden.

Start with the fine herbs, all six of them, fresh sprigs if they are available or the dried ones in neat little jars will do very well.

Keep in your refrigerator several nice earthen pots with tight covers and keep in these earthen pots the secret of your first herb success: *Herb Butter.* It is simple but it does the trick.

HERB BUTTER

The butter must be unsalted. Unsalted butter keeps its butterfat intact, while salted butter develops a watery fluid which the herbs refuse. Their fragrance is produced by their fine oils. Herb butter gives the final and exquisite touch to string beans, peas, spinach, asparagus, broccoli, mushrooms, Brussels sprouts, and many other vegetables. This butter is a definite improvement to all kinds of broiled meats and fish; it is unexpectedly delicate on steaks, broiled chicken and fish which really depend on herb butter (mixed with some lemon juice) to bring out their best flavors.

Fresh butter can be mixed with any one of the small groups of the fine herbs; it can be just as successfully mixed with any one of the single herbs such as basil, chervil, tarragon, thyme, rosemary, and chive. These mixtures are excellent for sandwich spreads and for vegetables. There is a favorite mixture of butter with wild marjoram, winter savory, and ground juniper berries to be used on heavy meats and game. Dill butter is exquisite for veal and fish, lobster, shrimp, or crabmeat.

Butter mixed with sweet marjoram does wonders to broiled lamb chops, and its flavor is a delicate surprise with scalloped potatoes; it makes of pork chops a festive dish.

Herb butter can be a study in itself and gives a wide field to the cook because there are—especially for heavy meats and roasts—the robust herbs as well as the fine ones for blending. The former when mixed with butter and applied in the final stage of roasting give unexpected improvements and surprises.

Herb butter should be mixed in the following proportion: Use two ounces of butter with one tablespoon very finely cut (with scissors) or chopped green herbs, or one-half teaspoon of dried herbs. The butter should be creamed and a few drops of lemon juice added. If dried herbs are used add before serving (for looks and flavor) some finely cut chive, or parsley, or even a few raw spinach leaves. Seasoning with salt and pepper or paprika should be applied shortly before serving.

Never top broiled foods with herb butter when still under the flame—it would immediately scorch the tender herb. Let the mixed butter melt over broiled meat or fish in the hot oven so that the herb flavors permeate the juices of fish or meat. Top cooked vegetables shortly before serving. Add mixed butter the size of a small nut for each serving, or two balls of herb butter if vegetables are served on the platter.

HERB BUTTER FOR BREAKFAST

I like to begin the day with something herbal. It is almost like a regime. It is refreshing to look at the greenness of herbs in the morning; above all, herbs relieve the monotony of eggs in flavor and in appearance.

The Boiled Egg. Into an egg cup place a small amount of herb butter (half a teaspoon—herb preference unlimited) and let the cup stand for a few minutes in the boiling water. Then break the egg into it over the butter.

The Fried Egg. The egg should have plenty of butter to "swim" in and fry slowly on a low heat. When ready, lift the fried egg from the pan to a plate, season and top it with the herb butter.

Scrambled Eggs. Scrambled eggs are made fluffier if one tablespoon of water is added to each egg when beating. Pour the mixture into a frying pan. Scrambled eggs, too, like to "assemble" in plenty of butter, hot but not sizzling. Top with herb butter more generously than the boiled or fried egg. Any one of these egg dishes may be served in the company of a few strips of bacon.

Omelet of Fine Herbs. This omelet is better when the

herbs are mixed with it before baking. For each egg one tablespoon of cold water; and before mixing the water in the eggs, a little flour (about as much as the point of a knife will hold for each egg) should be diluted, and egg and floured water lightly beaten to be just foamy. Season with salt and add paprika which should be like the touch of rouge on a woman's cheek. Now add finely cut herbs (any one of the three groups of the fine herbs will do—the choice being a personal one—with supplements of chive or parsley especially when dried herbs are used).

The one-egg omelet (and it turns out quite big and sufficient as a breakfast dish for one person) needs: one teaspoon of fresh herbs which include parsley or chive, or one-third of a teaspoon of dried herbs mixed with a dash of chive or parsley. Also sprinkle a bit of chive on the top of the finished omelet. Use a skillet with a low rim, about eight inches in diameter for a one-egg omelet. Spread butter generously in the pan and let it get hot, but not sizzling. Pour mixture into skillet. Watch the omelet, which should keep creamy on the inside. When the omelet is "settled" turn on heat rapidly to achieve a light brown crispness. Glide it onto a hot plate and fold the omelet twice. Crisp watercress on the plate is a very appetizing escort for the omelet.

The mixture for this omelet can be used in various ways. With the herbs may be mixed finely chopped ham or thinly sliced mushrooms, or (and this is a daring mixture and better used for luncheon) some grated onions, a dash of caraway seed, and chopped crisply cooked bacon. Also an omelet of fine herbs can be served with those very small sausages which usually are herb-minded too. Anybody will feel that with such a breakfast the day has made a very good beginning—and not burdensome either for the young digestion. These few examples will probably lead to many more interesting egg combinations according to the imagination and inventive spirit of the cook.

HERB BUTTER FOR SANDWICHES

Herb butter is a splendid accessory for parties such as tea or cocktails. Tidbits of toast, biscuit, or crackers spread with herb butters look as good as they taste.

There really is no end to the variety possible. Herb butter is delicious mixed with cheese and it will look very exotic with Roquefort or Gorgonzola or even Stilton, if a whiff of brandy is in the mixture. And then those, oh, very thin sandwiches of dark bread, not bigger than a silver dollar; or the "layer-cake" sandwiches with fillings alternating cheese and herb butter between slices of dark and white bread; to give still more color to the "cake" add one layer of a filling of grated sweet red pepper lightly mixed with finely chopped chive. Most piquant and extraordinarily good! What about a tiny baking-powder biscuit, hot, of course, split and filled with the mystifying green herb stuffing which melts in one's mouth. Or small biscuits stuffed with caviar mixed with chive and watercress; or with red caviar mixed with tarragon; or some square biscuits spread for a change with a green mayonnaise. And there is—and this one comes from my great-grandmother's charming old book —a small Napoleon-like *pâtisserie* with layers of herb custard instead of the sweet custard cream in layers.

The variety possible with herb butter mixtures is numerous and each one may be a novelty because each is individually conceived.

THE SAUCES

It is necessary before thinking of luncheon menus and dishes to take a second step in the knowledge of how to introduce herbs inconspicuously and with success. Herbs are gloriously masqueraded in sauces.

The short and long sauces, the hot and cold sauces—

they are all important, fundamental for the interesting *cuisine.* Herbs play a prominent part in sauces and in my opinion it is the herb that makes the sauce.

Once this knowledge is acquired the herbal world is opened to the novice; then from the cook's ingenuity will come about interesting and valuable new combinations. Every beginner in cooking knows something of the foundations for certain sauces. Indeed this white sauce foundation has become dangerously uniform. Usually it is a white paste-like, tasteless mixture of fats, flour, and milk. Herbs are too subtle to cope with the flavor of boiled milk or cream. (And it is an injustice to milk and cream to boil them!) In raw milk, because the cow feeds on grass and herbs, there can be a congeniality with herbs as there is in the mixture of butter and herbs. The foundation for some sauces consists of butter and flour mixed smoothly together. When heated and the butter begins to bubble in the pan, yellowing slowly together, the mixture is good in flavor and texture. This foundation which the French call *coulis* or *roux* can be thinned to great advantage with a light bouillon. (In my home not one drop of the water in which vegetables were cooked was ever thrown away.) The bouillons were kept in wide-necked bottles in a long row on a shelf in the cold room. One easily can understand the affinity of this combination: The butter, a product of herbs of the field, then the flour from the fruits of the field, then the vegetable essences; and when all this is blended, the herbs complete the fineness and delicacy of flavor of such a sauce.

There is no end to sauce possibilities—the fine herbs, the robust herbs, the transparent sauces, the sauces which should be velvety and those which should be very thick. There are several tricks for thickening sauces. Inexpensive and inoffensive is the thickening with potato flour—so little known in this country. Only one-half teaspoon of this flour is needed for enough sauce for chicken fricassee. The potato flour must be first diluted in a half cup of cold bouillon and stirred in while the sauce is boiling. Like a miracle the sauce thickens almost at once to the consistency the cook desires. Thickening with the yolk of an egg, to which sweet or sour cream and a few drops of lemon juice are added, is another European favorite. There also is the trick of using the water in which rice or barley cooked as either a thinning or thickening medium. These waters also substitute for the color of milk. Eggs used for thickening must be beaten separately in a bowl and the hot sauce poured over them. It also should be impressed upon the cook that herbs should be added to the sauce just a very few minutes before serving, because herbs unfold their fragrance within five minutes in the hot sauce.

To make *Sauce Hollandaise* perfect add a bouquet of any two herbs. In the famous *Sauce Béarnaise*—almost immortal—eggs, sweet butter, and seasoning are blended, and under constant beating more butter is added and in the end one tablespoon of fresh tarragon (or one-half teaspoon of dried tarragon mixed with one-half teaspoon of finely cut parsley) and one teaspoon of genuine tarragon vinegar to give the final touch. For this sauce the proportion of eggs to butter is two yolks to three tablespoons of butter at first, and then two tablespoons more of butter blended in just before the herbs.

The Green Sauces are enticing looking and can be exquisite in flavor. They are most accommodating and can be used for all kinds of light meats such as chicken, or left-overs of veal and fresh veal *ragoût,* too. But first of all for fish—especially fresh-water fish, and for shrimps, scallops, and crabmeat. A green sauce can be thinned with any kind of vegetable or chicken bouillon, depending on its use. It is preferable for fish to use a special bouillon of soup greens, onions, and one-half teaspoon of mixed spices prepared as the thinning bouillon. First, let the fish boil in this bouillon until tender and the fins can be removed. The bouillon is strained and then the herbs are added. For fish add finely chopped green dill and parsley, or parsley and marjoram, or parsley alone. The finishing touch for this dish is one-fourth teaspoon of lemon juice beaten with the yolk of an egg stirred with the bouillon.

Horseradish Sauce. The excellent horseradish root which is herb and spice at the same time is incredibly neglected in this country; it should be used without drenching it in vinegar. It must be grated when fresh. Sprayed with some lemon juice it will keep its virginal snowy whiteness. Freshly grated horseradish can of course be used just as it is, as a condiment when mixed with a few drops of lemon juice, one-half teaspoon of sugar, one tablespoon grated almonds. It can also be used in any kind of hot white sauce by grating the fresh horseradish, placing it in the sauce bowl and pouring the hot sauce over it. Horseradish must never boil. As a cold sauce it is mixed with whipped cream, faintly salted, and served cold for fish dishes or cold meats.

Sauce Ravigote. Boil a few shallots with vinegar and half a teaspoon of mixed spices until shallots are soft. Add this mixture to a strong white sauce (bouillon base); boil a few minutes longer and strain. After straining the sauce it must be returned to the pan when the green herbs, tarragon, chervil, finely chopped young spinach leaves, and a few leaves of French sorrel are added.

And again there are sauces which always are greatly improved and made interesting looking by adding any variety of herb butter.

Gravies look differently and taste refreshingly if finished with herb butter and some sweet or sour cream. Anchovy paste mixed with herb butter improves many roasts. For such uses the combinations are endless, once the cook has trained her own taste to the use of these seasonings.

It is great fun, the exploration of herbs. What a novelty it will be to your friends and what a pleasant *rencontre* to those who might renew some old acquaintance in such herb parades.

THE COLD SAUCES

Mayonnaise is the foundation of many of the cold sauces. First of all there is for an example the grand old sauce, the *Sauce Tartare.*

Sauce Tartare is a mayonnaise gone berserk. It goes in for all the fine herbs, chive included, and here they rub shoulders with some pretty strange company. Besides chive, there is the brave ancestor, the potential Spanish onion which has a say in this *Sauce Tartare*. There is even a whiff of garlic, grated with the onion. Finely chopped caper, followed by a teaspoon of anchovy paste, a dash of curry powder, a dash of cayenne, and finally French mustard intrudes too. Yet altogether they come to an understanding and the combination is very surprising. This kind of mayonnaise starts on a foundation of three hard-boiled egg yolks mashed, with one-half cup of oil (olive oil if possible); one teaspoon vinegar. To this the above herbs are added.

A very good and rather easy foundation for a *Sauce Tartare* is to beat in the upper part of a double boiler, over hot water, four yolks of eggs, two teaspoons of tarragon vinegar and four tablespoons of water until thick. Let sauce cool, beat in four tablespoons of oil, add the fine herbs, the chive, capers, anchovies, and as much of diluted English mustard powder as desired.

The *Rémoulade Indienne* is another one of those intriguing sauces which starts with a mayonnaise made of three hard-boiled egg yolks mashed fine, to which are added two tablespoons (altogether) finely chopped tarragon, origanum (wild marjoram), a few chopped spinach leaves, one tablespoon of English mustard powder, the juice of half a lemon, salt, a dash of *Indienne* pepper and one-fourth teaspoon of saffron or curry. Very festive for all meats, such as ham, roast beef or turkey, wild duck, and others.

Lobster Sauce. Make a mayonnaise of two egg yolks, finely cut chive and parsley and tarragon (two tablespoons of herbs altogether) and one teaspoon of finely chopped capers. Add the liquid of a small can of lobster and one teaspoon of French mustard. This sauce is to be mixed with the lobster only. Garnish the lobster with chopped watercress, endive French or green, diced cucumber, some thinly sliced raw mushrooms seasoned with salt and paprika and sprayed with a light French dressing.

FOR SALADS

Each one of the cold sauces can be used as an occasional salad dressing, yet the very simple salad dressing, of which herbs are such an important part, is the most desirable for the daily use of salads and indispensable for the variety of the green salads and lettuces.

To prepare the green salad according to the connoisseurs: The oil is placed in the bowl, then cut a clove of garlic in two pieces and toss into this oil; turn it around a little while, then add the herbs. This can be a very interesting procedure because the host, who of course is an expert in making *his* dressing, will involve his guests in argument about salads. This gives him time to play with the herbs in the oil, toss them around and around, until it is time to dismiss the garlic (ten or fifteen minutes). Each group of the fine herbs is excellent but not any one herb must play too prominent a part. You know, this is like a string quartet or quintet, an artistic submerging. Perhaps the host is fond of a little diluted mustard in the mixture or a *soupçon* of saffron or curry powder—it all depends on *his* mood. Finally, after the herbs are warmed in the oil, the argument stops abruptly and the host's absorption in his task begins; when you see him measure, with a reliable little spoon, the vinegar (from which positively he will first take a whiff), then the great moment has arrived. The crisp salad leaves will be tossed into the mixture with undulating movements. When there are other ingredients of the salad kind to be combined, such as tomato and cucumber, they are kept waiting in a separate bowl, and have been treated first to blend with the green salads: they have been seasoned, sprayed lightly with the same dressing. The guests look on fascinated and a solemn silence charges the atmosphere until the host smiles and heaves a light sigh of satisfaction.

Then the salad plates are filled with a kind of tenderness—oh, what a salad, really worth the performance! Of course this seldom is an American host—for what does his wife keep a regular *cordon bleu* (a female chef)! The salad must in this case be sent to the table ready-made, even if sometimes the gourmet host wrinkles his nose a little! I understand. I have seen American men cooking with a grim passion and a fierce temper. And amazingly good it was in their way, with sauces reeking of strong liqueurs (but they were good liqueurs) and condiments, and I never knew exactly what I ate but the little quails were genuine, or the lobsters *à la Newburg* were really lobsters!

I showed some American men how to make salads of a goodness they never knew about. The salads of lentils and beans and oriental dressings, and potato salad *à la Russe* with the fillets of herring and fresh caviar. And I served the salad of the celery root, topped them with all the fine herbs and a delicate transparent French dressing, golden yellow, and with all the greenness of the finely chopped herbs floating around. Perhaps it might interest some feminine readers to know that for fruit salad a superb dressing is made in which rosemary plays the big fiddle. This is very novel and interesting.

After all, it is worthwhile to know all the herbs and to

love them and know what they like and then to place them rightly. It takes time to specialize and it takes enthusiasm. But I wish, indeed fervently, that all these fine aromas of herbs and sauces and dressings would become the standard perfumes of the American kitchen—and the frying fumes less conspicuous.

CHAPTER FIVE

And, Oh, the Vegetables!

ONE OF MY GREAT JOYS is to walk through the markets and especially through that part where there is live food! The vegetable and fruit stalls in their abundance and colors are truly majestic and overpowering. All the blessed things to take home for health and fine taste—real feasts! The other day when a young painter friend followed me through the narrow multicolored alleys of the market, I picked up some celery roots which were exhibiting themselves in their solid earthen color and their crown of stanch green leaves.

"What are they for?" she asked a little timidly. I gasped. This young friend of mine never had heard of them. So I invited her to have a celery-root salad with me. And she didn't know fennel—the *finocchio*—either. And she passed by many wonderfully good, brave vegetables, yet she stood entranced before all the cabbages—their noble cousin the cauliflower included. A little pyramid of carrots made a charming background for the cauliflower, and right snug to this throned a pear-shaped eggplant—*l'aubergine* as the French call it. (Aubergine has long been the name of the warm purple, one of the most interesting colors for luxurious silks and velvets.) And I had to tell my friend about the leeks, which give zest to potato soup and always are there when the bouillon otherwise would lack "this something" that never can be prescribed until one finds it—just the right touch.

THE STRING BEAN

String beans are the most misunderstood and tormented of vegetables. Their fine flavor, their green, velvety beauty are completely annihilated by the usual methods of cooking them. Frequently they are sacrificed on the altar of a leg of mutton or ham. Beans readily absorb flavors, and as both mutton and ham are very arrogant this bean, when cooked with them, has not the slightest chance to assert its own personality. Fully understood, string beans are most delicate, and in company with a bouquet of summer savory or basil or marjoram they respond most happily.

String beans should be picked when very young. Drop the washed beans into enough boiling water to barely cover. A bouquet (three or four sprigs) of fresh summer savory (or a teaspoon of dried summer savory tied in a little cloth bag to two pounds of beans) should be thrown in the water a short while before the tiny whole beans get into this steaming fragrant bath. Cook fifteen minutes, lid off, letting water boil down. Add two tablespoons of butter and continue to cook slowly until beans are tender. Drain, keeping water for vegetable stock. Salt to taste and put back on stove to evaporate for two minutes. Shake, heap on platter, and top with sweet butter to which finely chopped parsley and basil have been added. The varieties of beans which are not as young should have strings removed and be cut in strips and treated the same way.

When boiling very stout string beans with meats, first remove strings and break them in square pieces; then add to the meat stock when the meat is almost done. The bean flavor will then be preserved and it will also add to the fineness of the meat. Don't forget a bouquet of fresh summer savory or some of the dried herbs tied in a little cheesecloth bag and added for a few minutes to this pot.

THE CABBAGES

The cabbages are the best and tastiest vegetables if only rightly interpreted. Cabbage must have its water bath thoroughly perfumed with caraway seed and with a dash of wild marjoram. Green cabbage, cut in thick slices and slowly boiled in such a water, to which a little salt is also added, is a grand dish. Carefully placed on the plate or platter, it should be richly covered with Parmesan cheese and hot butter; or with herb butter of thyme, sweet marjoram, or a mixture of tarragon and chive. This is very good. Or serve the cabbage snowed under a cover of Parmesan cheese with the herb butter on top.

Stuffed cabbage looks pompous, but when the stuffing is seasoned with sage or sweet marjoram and Tellicherry pepper it is an interesting dish. I prefer a mixture of chopped cooked lamb with sweet marjoram as a stuffing for the cabbage. Of course cole slaw has a prominent place in the culinary world, and that should be. With an herbal dressing it is delicious; or a light mayonnaise with a bit of *tartare* influence.

The purple cabbage is best steamed with butter and parsley in a very little water. Red cabbage is delicious if accompanied by chestnuts, and a dash of caraway seed. (The latter is said to help a tender digestion.) The chestnuts should be precooked in water, peeled and added to the cabbage as soon as it is put in to cook. Season with salt and a dash of cayenne pepper.

THE LENTIL

The lentil is the little brunet bean to which I am very partial—because once it almost saved my life. I must tell this story because it may be needed to convince you of the value of the lentil; and especially it may help growing youngsters to trust lentils and eat them at least twice a week. The little bean, which contains phosphate, was prescribed for me when I was studying in Paris—very young—and had overtaxed my strength. The solemn French *medico* came always in black gloves, left a little slip on the table, ordering a glass of Dubonnet before dinner and a daily course of lentils. And it is from that time that I knew the value and the goodness of lentil soup—the bouillon was an extract of this richly endowed bean, cooked down and strained. Origanum (wild marjoram) should always be cooked with the lentils.

THE CARROT

So delicate is this vegetable that it is predestined by nature just to be taken from its cool ground and eaten right on the spot, crisp and fresh. Yet if you take it home and cook it, then please don't scrape this lovable-looking rosy thing of its charm. Just place it in a little boiling water. After a while the skin comes off easily and the carrot underneath looks just as alluring as in its original state. And if it is served dressed with melted fresh herb butter, that is all there is to it. Any kind of fine herbs, chive, chervil, or even parsley, is very good with fresh-looking carrots which have not come from the steam bath stripped and anæmic looking. And by the way, the water in which the carrots cooked is good to drink, or used for making soup; creamed carrot soup with lots of greens in it is the second best way to serve this vegetable.

THE CAULIFLOWER

Cauliflower is often mistreated, cooked from all its virginal glory to a grayish-looking, soft, mushy thing, its youthfulness ruined. In the cooking pot, cauliflower only wants to have its heavy stalk wet. Let the cauliflower sit on its trunk in water just that deep. Keep the cover on the cooking pot, not because of the cauliflower vapors permeating the house—this too is not the fault of the cauliflower, but the fault of the cook. Cauliflower must simmer or steam, the fine border of green leaves must never be removed. Cauliflower as cooked in my kitchen has no time to develop the cabbagy perfume. It is quickly tender and ready to serve.

Cauliflower expands under an herb sauce—and the fine old Hollandaise, rejuvenated with some tarragon or sweet marjoram is really very good for this. Bread crumbs fried in unsalted butter and sprinkled with parsley on the cooked cauliflower make a delicious dish; so it is with Parmesan cheese, simply grated and warmed with *beurre noir* (butter that melts in the oven to a golden brown and gets a dash of tarragon vinegar). Cauliflower is a good addition to the salad bowl, its little flowers mixed, *uncooked,* amongst fresh green salad with a good herb dressing.

THE CELERY ROOT

I wish to get back to the celery root. Bleached celery, so conspicuous in the markets, has not only outmoded celery root but has made of it the forgotten vegetable. Yet there is room for both in the *cuisine;* celery root must be cooked to bring out all its refreshing and fine flavor, while bleached celery loses its crisp qualities when subjected to cooking, although braised it is delicious. The root of celery should be seriously reinstalled, not only because it is a versatile and solid vegetable of exceptional flavor but it is said to have medicinal qualities. The root of the celery, and some of its strongly scented leaves, cooked in a meat bouillon are most effective. They give the bouillon a "strong support." This flavor blends splendidly with parsley root which also has been neglected. Scrape the rough-looking celery root, clean it thoroughly, and parboil it; but only until its skin can be slipped off, and there appears the white soul of the celery—most presentable. Spray with lemon juice immediately to prevent its turning dark. If celery root is to be served hot, cut it in slices, return it to very little of the cooking water, add butter and let it slowly simmer until tender. This is the braising mentioned above. Season with salt and freshly grated pepper, with chive, parsley, or chervil butter, and a dash of lemon juice. A little white sauce thickened with sour cream and paprika is a good addition to this.

Celery root makes an excellent purée. After peeling, replace the root in the cooking water and continue to boil until very soft. Mix this purée with finely chopped chive and sweet butter.

Don't forget celery-root salad. Here celery becomes an aristocrat. Parboil first and then peel, boil again with some lemon juice added to the water. When tender (not soft) spear each root on a fork and cut in thin strips. While it is still warm, marinate it with olive oil and let it stand for a while. Then pour only the dressing over it

—the beloved French dressing without garlic. Tarragon is the most congenial herb for celery root, and finely chopped parsley is essential to complement the celery flavor. Season with salt and the Tellicherry pepper. For enlivening the color scheme sprinkle some of the beautifully rouging paprika over it. Watercress is a most harmonious garnish or addition to the plate.

Bleached white celery used raw is too well-known to need comment here.

THE SPINACH

With Lent comes spinach. This green is eaten mostly with a respectful shudder because there is a great legend about spinach and the iron it contains. Some scientific luminary has torn down this legend; spinach can be something more exciting than a health asset. I believe that the bad reputation of spinach does not lie with the spinach but with the cooks who mostly are at a loss to make this vegetable palatable. In Italy I once got an idea of a really palatable spinach. Let us call this dish Italian Spinach. After washing and washing spinach, place it in a paper towel to drain. For two pounds of spinach melt one-fourth pound of fresh butter in a casserole, add half a cup of olive oil, cut one onion in half and bring butter, oil, and onion to the boiling point; add the spinach gradually, sprinkle with salt and pepper and when all is in the casserole, cook for forty minutes on very low heat. This should be until the spinach is freed from water and has absorbed the butter and the oil. With a fork turn the spinach carefully and frequently, dismiss the onion, and serve. The Italians always sprinkle their cooked spinach with Parmesan cheese. It is astonishing how the spinach mellows with this treatment.

I learned to like spinach cooked in the company of Romaine. In strongly boiling salted water this combination takes only ten minutes to reach the right point for being placed in the strainer. (I prefer it passed through the strainer instead of chopping.) Two pounds of puréed spinach and Romaine will absorb one-eighth pound of butter when placed in a casserole for fifteen minutes. Five minutes before serving add one-half cup of cream and another eighth pound of butter by-and-by in small pieces. Salt and pepper to taste. With this, garnish either with fried croutons, or, if the spinach is a separate course, it can be accompanied by oyster plant fried in a batter.

Spinach soufflé is a delicious luncheon dish. To make it, clean the pound of spinach and cook it rapidly in boiling salt water. After ten minutes drain it and pass it through the strainer. Mix it with one cup of Béchamel sauce and grated Parmesan cheese. Beat the yolks of four eggs; beat the whites stiff; add one tablespoon of finely chopped parsley, chive, and rosemary. Blend with spinach mixture and bake in a deep oven-glass dish in hot oven for twelve minutes.

THE OYSTER PLANT

The oyster plant should be more popular; it has many possibilities. To cook it, clean it, parboil it, and then strip it of its brownish skin. (This vegetable is called *scorzo nero* in Italy.) When stripped of its outer skin it has a fine complexion which immediately must be treated with some lemon juice. The long roots can be cut in round or long slices and placed in a casserole with butter and a few spoonfuls of water, to oven-cook for the final tenderness. Salt and paprika are added; parsley and tarragon are the herbs which give the last touch, and a dash of sour cream gives a velvety coat to this delicate vegetable.

Oyster plant also can be parboiled, stripped of the brown skin, sprayed with lemon juice and then rolled in a mixture of finely chopped parsley, tarragon, or the dry herbs mixed with parsley and a few drops of olive oil. It is a kind of marinade and the vegetable should have an hour to absorb the herb fragrance. Then these pieces are dipped in a beer batter: this is a very delicate batter made of one-fourth pound of sifted flour, one tablespoon of olive oil, and one cup beer with the stiffly beaten whites of two eggs. Fry in deep hot fat or in a pan in butter till golden brown.

Oyster plant, boiled and skinned, also makes an extremely fine salad sprinkled with chive and tarragon and a well-seasoned French dressing. Watercress is the congenial green addition.

THE CUCUMBER

While eating cucumbers I think of one summer in Finland, that land of a thousand lakes and islands—private islands with the sea waves as a protective wall. To this blessed isolation even neighbors could not "run in"—they had to swim in. What wonderful eaters the Nordics are! With breakfast the daily round of culinary stunts began. What puzzled me at first at this meal was that amidst the abundance of cereals, cheeses, and smoked all-kinds-of-things, was an enormous bowl of freshly cubed cucumbers. And right there I received a little but very illuminating lecture: the cucumber is the hot summer vegetable *par excellence* in Russia, and Finland is very close to Russia. They eat it as a fruit and they eat it as a vegetable, and in salad and soup. Cucumber is thirst quenching, cooling, contains plenty of mineral salts, and is the best inside and outside remedy for the complexion. Who then wouldn't begin the day eating cucumbers, if for nothing else but their beautifying qualities?

Cucumbers have a delicious flavor when their idiosyncrasies are respected. If they are drenched in vinegar and salt they are drained of their vital juices, robbed of their charm and left a limp, colorless pulp on the plate—nothing but a most indigestible martyred vegetable. Cucumbers want herbs; and they should never be eaten in the wake of a big meal. They are among the finest appetizers, not only for the Nordic people but for every gourmet in the world. There is the cucumber in the nude—bejeweled only with the fine herbs, as many as the cook can find; but the most piquant cucumber is prepared with green dill cut to atoms and simply mixed in with the seasoning of salt and pepper. This is a last minute affair, because salt remaining too long on the cucumber ruins its value. Then there is cucumber in cubes, salt and green dill mixed with sour cream and mixed together, the whole thing very cold, just served as curtain raiser or for cold buffets or at a light supper with cold cuts!

THE EGGPLANT

There is a strange change which the beautiful *aubergine,* or eggplant, undergoes without its purple coat: it becomes a helpless looking affair and very few people know what to do with it. Fried, of course, it seems to lose still more of its character, or has eggplant no character and no especial value? It is a social plant: give it the right company, green pepper for instance, and sauté it in olive oil with some of the Tellicherry pepper, add to this combination a few slices of Bermuda onions, and the eggplant will expand and develop a fine, subtle flavor which will help its associates as much as they help the eggplant. Cut the vegetable in cubes, with the green peppers cut in strips and the onions in rings; beginning with two tablespoons of oil, two tablespoons of water, paprika —just a generous dash—covered and placed on a low fire the three flavors will blend splendidly; one tablespoon of freshly cut basil (one-half teaspoon of dried basil) and this trio of vegetables will always interest the connoisseur; it is a good companion for lamb chops or broiled fish of any kind.

Fried eggplant begins with thick slices of the peeled vegetable lightly sprayed with lemon juice, salt and white pepper (freshly grated if possible); then the slices are dipped in a batter and fried in deep hot fat. The fat should be butter or oil. I remember the excellent eggplant dish I ate in Rapallo on the Italian Riviera. It was a beautiful dish and whenever I serve it now, it is a hit. The eggplant is cut in thick, round slices (don't soak it in salt water—the little bitter taste is an asset). Sprinkle some lemon juice over the slices with rosemary and marjoram; salt very lightly, dust them solidly with flour and have butter in the skillet very hot (not brown); fry them two minutes on one side and two minutes on the other side. Bed them on a slice of toast (whole wheat rusk if possible), top the eggplant with a little chopped spinach in sour cream, and chive; top this with a thick slice of ripe red tomato sprinkled with chive and a few drops of oil. Pour over the whole a thick Parmesan cheese sauce. This makes a wonderful luncheon, and a very popular Lenten dish, especially in Latin countries. Call it *Eggplant de luxe.*

THE GREEN PEPPER

Green peppers are very interesting when cut in strips and braised with onions, in olive oil, seasoned with salt and paprika and a dash of cayenne. They must be the hot variety and the green peppers must be interspersed with some of the red ones. This is delicious with roast beef or steaks.

Green peppers stuffed are greatly misunderstood. For them there should be a fish stuffing; or a stuffing of cottage cheese mixed with raisins, parsley finely cut, and tarragon, and highly seasoned. The contrast of flavors is surprising and good. Also they are good stuffed with chopped boiled ham and rice with Parmesan cheese and a dash of omelet herbs and chive.

There are many combinations but please avoid the bread stuffing, onions, and the use of left-overs in green peppers! I tried once a mixture of chicken livers and mushrooms, finely chopped, and a little piece of sweetbread all sautéed together with fresh butter, lemon juice, finely chopped parsley, a dash of sweet marjoram, a few green peas. A few drops of port wine added to the mixture made a noble combination. I served these in a ring of oriental rice. The dish was a little sensation. And a very agreeable one for luncheon.

THE TURNIP

There is the very humble turnip, so strangely attired, so demure looking but with a flavor quite its own. The

French found this out in marvelous dishes. Yet there was a turnip dish on our table at home which came from that diary of my great-grandmother. She confessed she was at odds as to what to do with this stable vegetable. But she found ways. Use the turnip when very young, parboil it unpeeled with a few caraway seeds. After ten minutes remove turnips, peel, and place in a casserole. Add to six turnips three tablespoons of sour cream, one-half teaspoon of dried basil, one teaspoon of freshly cut basil and cook them covered in the oven twenty minutes. Season with salt and paprika and a dash of lemon juice. The result is surprising.

For turnip purée larger turnips can be used, yet beware of the woody ones. Parboil unpeeled in water with caraway seed, peel after ten minutes and return to water until very tender, mash with fresh unsalted butter (be generous); when serving, place in the center a mound of shredded onions which have been stewing with parsley and butter and a few drops of lemon juice. The mound must be very green looking; better add a few finely chopped raw spinach leaves before serving.

I have learned to appreciate the rutabaga, a yellow Swedish turnip; when baked, unpeeled, in the oven and served cut open with fresh butter and lots of parsley and a dash of lemon juice, it is delicious.

THE BRUSSELS SPROUT

Brussels sprouts make a delicate dish if in the first boiling water thyme has been permitted to be company to the sprouts; and as this vegetable belongs to the cabbage family it must have a little bag of caraway seed also assisting it to be sociable. The finest way of serving Brussels sprouts is with herb butter made of sweet marjoram and parsley—thyme is too strong here, besides, it has done its job in the cooking. Parmesan cheese sprinkled over Brussels sprouts, or hot parsley butter poured over them, makes them delicious and adds to the appearance. Brussels sprouts, of course, have to be rather underdone so as to lose nothing of their refreshing greenness.

THE BROCCOLI

Broccoli, this "black" cauliflower which grows wild in the Italian *campagna* has become a great favorite in America—but only to be misunderstood for the most part. As with cauliflower it is necessary to keep the "flower" out of the water, otherwise this part is cooked to pieces before the stems are tender. The herbs to be boiled with broccoli should be a little bag of caraway seed—for the sake of tender digestions—and a little sprig of wild marjoram.

THE SQUASH

Of the squash family, the Italian squash or *zucchi* is the most delicate. This is a vegetable of a very subtle nature. The *zucchis* of a soft dark green are never peeled; cut lengthwise they are decorative and, as they originated in Italy, they prefer being treated with olive oil, lemon and a bit of salt and pepper. When half done they should be supported by finely chopped parsley and a generous dash of wild marjoram. In such treatment the *zucchis* gain courage and the wild marjoram automatically coöperates with their fine flavor. The final touch for the *zucchis* is a sprinkling with grated Parmesan cheese.

Among the squash which I learned to know in America I prefer the cymling (white scalloped squash) which is cut in half and cooked in the oven with a stuffing of butter, Parmesan cheese and basil. Hubbard squash cooked, mashed, and seasoned with cinnamon and freshly grated dark pepper is an interesting and most agreeable vegetable. Any of these simple vegetables of strong flavor is delicious if when cooked it is helped with sour cream and thyme, basil, or chive. And if time is pressing, any one of them may be simply cooked in salt water, mashed and topped with any kind of herb butter and lemon juice.

THE POTATO

And finally there is the potato. This vegetable doesn't excite many cooks and so it is seldom shown in the various delicious garbs it may wear. How beautiful potatoes look as potato soufflé! Like the finest confectioner's work. In this dish one can easily realize the splendid caliber of the potato. Pages could be written on the potato and its close affiliation with herbs and spices; potatoes and parsley and chives are almost inseparable. Also, potatoes should never be boiled without caraway seeds and they should always be boiled in the jacket. Much of the nutriment value and flavor of the potato is lost when peeled. For finishing touches the cooked potatoes can be taken from their caraway seed bouillon when half done. Then the peelings are easily removed. One very popular and successful dish is made with half-cooked potatoes. (Save the water of the potato in which they have been boiling primarily.) In a casserole a Bermuda onion, a few tablespoons of finely cut parsley and three tablespoons of butter are stewing leisurely; add to this the peeled and sliced potatoes (not too thin), cover with a little of the strained potato water, add salt to taste; continue cooking till potatoes are done. Another variation on this same recipe is to add the potatoes to the onion, parsley, and butter, and cover them with milk, seasoning them with a good deal of paprika. Simmer till tender.

There are many delicious potato "pastes." Pancakes of raw potatoes, the marjoram potatoes, and the soufflés.

Potato Pancake. Grate four big raw potatoes, press out excess water. Add four egg yolks, salt to taste, one heaping tablespoon flour, two to three tablespoons sour cream. Mix well together. Beat four egg whites thoroughly and blend with the mixture. Drop into frying pan and fry slowly in very hot butter, like small pancakes.

This same recipe may be simplified by beating all four eggs together. The result is good, though somewhat less elegant than the first method.

Potato Soufflé. Cut slices of raw potatoes, not too thin. Throw into deep fat which should be very hot and a golden brown color. When potatoes are slightly yellow remove them to paper toweling. Then reheat the fat and throw potatoes in again; they will puff out on this second cooking, like small balloons. They must be watched carefully and removed as they puff out.

Potatoes are high in nutriment value and many nations make this vegetable their mainstay. The Swiss people, for instance, begin their day with a national dish ot potatoes, called *roesti.* They cook potatoes in the jacket, peel them and put them in shallow fat to be browned. They eat them with their native herb cheese. This is not only for the poor people; it is everybody's dish. A breakfast without *roesti* is a mistake. This does not prevent them from having potatoes again for the main meal of the day. Potatoes must be on the table, and the Swiss people are famed for endurance and fine minds—the potato supplements the national dish of cheese and milk. The Slavic people, especially the Bohemians and Slovak or the Hungarian, used to have, at least once a day, a substantial meal of potatoes in some form or another.

Then there are the aristocrats among the vegetables, such as asparagus, mushrooms, artichokes, the okras, the green peas. Those vegetables need no disguise; each has such a grand individual *noblesse* of flavor; and it is with these that the herb butters are of wonderful service. They really enhance the exquisite flavors of these super-vegetables. They have always been served separately in well-planned menus, all by themselves, and suspense precedes their entry.

The variety of dishes possible with vegetables is enormous if they are treated with the same interest given rare meats or fowl. They really are worth it and a *cuisine* that excels in fine vegetable combinations always excels in variety. Vegetables can be salads and the salad greens can be served as vegetables.

After all, one has to learn to know what associate would please the vegetable, and experience is the best teacher. There is no question but that the great surprises always lie with the vegetables and salads which accompany the meat. Attention should be paid to the fact that *ragoûts* should always be accompanied by a vegetable treated only with herb butter, and sparingly. If the *ragoût* includes vegetables cooked with it then no separate vegetable should be served. The true value of each dish is lessened in such a case, while if served separately each is important. In my childhood home, vegetables were usually served separately from meats—unless there were cold cuts. These are a good background for the full flavor of vegetables.

CHAPTER SIX

Meats, Poultry, and Game

MEATS, POULTRY, AND GAME present a great field for using herbs. To treat meats with an herb marinade is a modern version of the ancient secret of the veneration of meats. In the Bible, and in the oldest scripts of all the peoples on earth, one reads and wonders about the sacrifices and the rituals of the animals on the altar to the gods. After an animal was slaughtered it was drenched in precious wines and rubbed with aromatic herbs and spices and then barbecued. People have forgotten the ancient rites, of course, but nevertheless they still love to barbecue their meats (usually minus spices and herbs), especially since there is a grill in their own kitchens gleaming with modernity. Yet the meat, fowl, and game go unperfumed, although herbs are still growing everywhere and there are the many spices from all over the world. And yet this process of ennobling foods should be reinstalled, for herbs and spices and fine oils and lemon juices are much more than a ritual. They tenderize, they add zest for the palate, and in some cases counteract certain acids.

The marinading of the meats is really the correct preparation for cooking meats, and such marinades do the work of flavoring much better than all the stuffing in the world. The foundation of a good marinade is the herbs of both groups, the fine herbs as well as some of the robust ones. If the herbs are dried they should be steeped in warm olive oil for a few minutes; when they are freshly cut the chopping releases the fine oils from the herbs. In any marinade the combination of herbs, spices, and berries is tied together by the oil and the juices of the lemon. The marinade varies with the meat. From the pages of my ancestor's diary I give the experienced and proven marinades. Before placing in the marinade, the meat is cleansed outside and inside by rubbing with the inside of a lemon.

BEEF

The Marinade. For beef marinade use finely cut borage, origanum (wild marjoram), sweet onion (Bermuda), one clove of garlic, chopped celery leaves and parsley, freshly grated white or black pepper, lemon juice, and olive oil. This mixture does not look unlike French dressing and the quantity is according to the poundage of the meat.

For roast beef or prime rib roast cut incisions between the ribs, and the marinade is smoothed in without salting the meat. Beef, when marinated, can be rolled in wax paper and left in the refrigerator for twenty-four hours. This beef marinade can be most successfully used for the pot roasts, stews, or goulash, but not boiled beef, which is boiled in vegetables and herbs and receives its flavor while cooking.

Cooking the Beef. The marinade can be removed before cooking. (I always leave it in and remove only the garlic.) The meat is then seasoned with salt, pepper or paprika, the top brushed with olive oil and then placed in the oven at a very low heat (250–300° F.) for two and one-half hours (or more) without water or fat of any kind. (This slow cooking process incidentally is the newest and most reliable formula of the Bureau of Home Economics of the United States Department of Agriculture.) No basting is done; the meat does not shrink. On the contrary it expands, and the cook is sure of the roast. The juices of the roast beef develop under the influence of the marinade to an exquisite gravy which can be strained but needs no additional thickening.

Such a piece of beef needs the proper *entourage*. I recommend a horseradish sauce, warm, the one with freshly grated horseradish in a bowl over which is poured the sauce made of cream and grated almonds and a few drops of lemon juice; potatoes that bake while the roast is in the oven and are treated with parsley butter tinted with paprika and coarse salt; vegetables (but not creamed ones).

Pot roast is treated with the same marinade, yet instead of making incisions it should be larded all around —the bacon strips rolled in the same marinade, and the rest of the marinade placed at the bottom of the pot from the beginning of the cooking. The various vegetables and potatoes, everything cut in squares, should be added only after one and one-half hours of roasting. Oven temperature the same as for roast beef is maintained, and after two or two and one-half hours the cook will remove the lid and find a perfect dish. Do not forget to season the pot roast thoroughly with salt and freshly grated pepper. And as I think back to my childhood home I remember that the additional and influential robust herb which always made the pot roast still more delicate was borage; a fresh or dry sprig will do the trick.

LAMB

The Marinade. Sweet marjoram, thyme, caraway seed, parsley, onion, garlic, oil and lemon juice. Again incisions are made if it is the saddle of lamb, and the marinade is placed as explained in the rib roast. The excess fat should be removed, especially from the top of the leg of lamb. To help the fine flavor and to keep the fat under control, the larding with bacon is highly recommended, especially if the bacon strips are first rolled in the marinade. I leave the marinaded lamb for twenty-four hours (protected by wax paper) in the refrigerator. If the lamb has grown into mutton, its chops should be in the marinade for six hours before broiling. Lamb for *ragoût* or stewed lamb should stay in the marinade for twelve hours. For the latter, cut the meat into squares and place the marinade, and garlic too, with the stew from the beginning. Season with salt, pepper or paprika.

Cooking the Lamb. As with the roast beef, the leg or saddle of lamb should be left in the marinade during the cooking process. The meat must be well seasoned, the excess fat, especially the whole fat cover, removed, the leg larded and the saddle simply wrapped in bacon strips. The bacon should be more on the lean than on the fat side. Make it again the rule to place oven heat at 250° F., and leave the roast without additional water to develop its tasty qualities undisturbed. No bastings. The surprise is great when after two to two and one-half hours or more the most delicious juices are in the bottom of the pan. Add a few spoonfuls of sour cream to the juices, mix and serve with the roast.

Chops. Mutton or lamb chops taken out of the marinade and broiled slowly under a low flame will develop all the aromas of their herb treatment. When finished on both sides and ready to be served, make a solid ball of unsalted butter mixed with anchovy paste and finely cut chives; don't season the butter if mixed with anchovy. However, mix salt and paprika with the butter if you are using fresh dill, sweet marjoram, or tarragon; if the herbs are dried always intermingle green parsley or chive or finely cut spinach leaves to keep the illusion of fresh herbs. The aromas are perfectly preserved in dried herbs.

Lamb Stew. The meat, before it is cut in squares, should be placed in the marinade. And again after cutting, do not separate the marinade from the meat but let them all stew together (including bones) very slowly, while some finely cut bacon, some more onions, carrots, and turnips cut in small cubes are added after an hour; potatoes still a little later. The meat and vegetables in a stew should not be a negligible medley, but a good thing to eat and look at. Before serving, sprinkle with finely cut parsley.

PORK

The Marinade. Marinade makes the pork; it changes completely the somewhat arrogant individuality of pork and changes it to such a point that my friends eat cold pork thinking it is turkey! I respect the individual flavor of the meats I prepare, yet modification or elevation is a wonderful thing. Being well groomed does not affect the characteristics of people either; it rather brings out their best points. The marinade for pork varies a trifle from those for other meats—it must be subtle, not emphasize, but subdue somewhat the pork characteristics. Therefore a marinade is made of onions or shalots mixed with a lot of parsley, half a teaspoon of powdered caraway seed, a whiff of dry thyme or a sprig of fresh thyme, a whiff of dry basil or a few crushed leaves, and the usual addition of lemon juice and olive oil. When the roast is half done a good rubdown with sweet marjoram is a great asset.

Cooking Pork. Pork before roasting should be rid of its excess fat. It is the dripping of too much fat into the cooking meat which makes pork indigestible. Pork should never be larded, and the incisions for the marinade should be deep, and the marinade retained during roasting.

With the marinade retained and before the meat is placed in the oven, rub some ground caraway seed into the pork roast and add one fresh onion, cut in half, to the pan. Season thoroughly. Don't omit the oven rule of 250° F., but look into the oven after an hour to see if the fat in the pan is excessive; if so, simply spoon off some of it. And in the last half hour of roasting, add potatoes, which are splendid for absorbing some of the fat in the pan.

Pork Chops can be treated in diminutive proportions the same way. It is difficult to bring pork chops to the table just right—they are so easily under or over-done. Cook them for a while on low heat (having cut off the side fat). Have some olive oil in the pan, which does not burn and fill the kitchen with infernal fumes. Rub both sides of the chop with lemon juice and sweet marjoram and a few seeds of caraway. When the chops are done place herb or anchovy or garlic butter on the top. Dill butter is excellent with chops and I call these chops *de luxe*. Cooked lentils are delicious with pork chops; so is spinach. But do not serve sauerkraut with them, for it does not help their flavor.

VEAL

The Marinade. Veal is a bland-flavored meat and needs pepping up. The marinade is particularly good for this kind of meat, and veal responds extraordinarily well to treatment. As a paradox I like best for veal the marinade employed for game. The juniper berry brings an interesting aroma to certain herbs and especially to the onion in the marinade. Try this marinade: one tablespoon of crushed juniper berries, one grated turnip, one grated carrot, one teaspoon of dried thyme, a few celery leaves, one tablespoon of Italian parsley, half a Bermuda onion cut finely, two shallots, the juice of half a lemon, two tablespoons of olive oil. Leave meat in marinade for twenty-four hours. This marinade is very effective with the tenderloin of veal, the *côtelette* part and veal kidney (freed from its heavy fat). The same marinade should be used for the leg of veal or for the breast of veal before it is stuffed. It really is an enhancement of the veal taste—as if the veal suddenly came of age, still keeping its fine milky taste of the young animal.

Tenderloin of Veal. When taken from the marinade keep some of it between the ribs; it helps the juices amalgamate with the marinade. Veal takes very well to bacon. Before being blanketed with bacon strips the top should be rubbed with salt and paprika (which is more congenial to veal than pepper) and sprinkled with finely cut parsley and chervil, the greens protected by the bacon cover. Season with salt and paprika between the ribs but leave the kidney alone; it is allergic to salt and immediately shrinks and gets tough. Roast in a slow oven (250-300° F.) like all the other roasts without the addition of water or basting.

The leg of veal can be treated the same way, only instead of covering the top with bacon strips, lard it with bacon cut in fine long strips, dipped in the marinade from which the leg of veal has been taken, and seasoned with salt and paprika.

To the gravy of both the tenderloin of veal and the leg can be added, fifteen minutes before serving, a few tomatoes, fresh or canned, and a few tablespoons of sour or sweet cream. If sweet cream is used, add lemon juice to taste, and one teaspoon of anchovy butter.

There are the *côtelettes Viennese* which can be cut from the leg without harming the roast, and used for another occasion. These *côtelettes* should be very thin, really almost like a leaf. Sprinkle with tarragon and basil, season with salt and paprika, roll in flour, dip in beaten egg and tightly cover with fine bread crumbs; fry in deep fat rapidly to a light golden brown. Place first on blotting paper, then on a hot, dry platter. Adorn each *côtelette* with a rolled anchovy, topped with finely chopped capers. All green vegetables (not creamed) topped with herb butter are delicious with these chops; so are young potatoes with parsley.

Pilaff of veal. This is an excellent dish based on the oriental pilaff. The veal, cut into heavy squares, is stewed with finely cut bacon and an avalanche of cut sweet onions, sweet marjoram, lots of paprika and not too much salt until half done; rice is added with some additional water. The pilaff must not be liquid; it is rather pompously red and compact and very shiny. There are all kinds of combinations left to the imagination of the cook. Rosemary is a very interesting addition when added to any kind of veal.

I wish to mention still the veal chop. This is a *côtelette en nature,* rolled only in flour and braised in butter to a fine crusty brown, and treated with a *maître d'hôtel* sauce—lots of finely cut parsley and lemon juice; and served, topped with dill butter (green dill, finely cut, and mixed with unsalted butter).

POULTRY

Turkey, duck, goose, chicken, squab, etc., after being rid of feathers and stubbles, should be given a dry cleaning with lemon juice inside and outside. This makes for tenderness and flavor. And the marinade makes the fowl.

Turkey Marinade. Chopped carrots, olives, onions and garlic, half a dozen cloves, thyme, parsley, rosemary, olive oil and lemon juice. If the turkey is to be stuffed the marinade should be removed entirely. Leave the turkey in the marinade for twenty-four hours. The turkey now undergoes an entirely different treatment after marinading. Most fowl is in the habit of having its cavity stuffed. It is a good habit, too, yet it has grown so stereotyped and monotonous that to have to look at the traditional turkey in the season is almost a calamity. It should not be that way, with all the possibilities at hand for arousing the cook's imagination. Fowl must have the advantage of being pre-treated, and one cannot make a subtle stuffing in sufficient bulk to fill the cavity of an eighteen-pound turkey. The under-the-skin stuffing is scarcely known in this country, yet it is unique and practical.

Let me hand down to you some of that knowledge and you may do what you want—improve it, embellish it, accept it, or dismiss it. One of the unusual stuffings for this purpose is that of chestnuts cooked and puréed and mixed with mushrooms. After one pound of mushrooms have been peeled use the heads and stems, steam in a glass of Madeira, let cool and grind them with the liver of the bird. Place the mixture for several hours in the refrigerator to blend. Then mix with one pound of chestnuts which have been boiled, peeled, and purèed. Add one-fourth pound of finely chopped bacon, one-half teaspoon each of chopped origanum, chervil, and parsley. Add one teaspoon in all of the four spices—powdered cloves, nutmeg, cinnamon, and ginger. Season with salt and a dash of Tellicherry pepper. Instead of pushing this delicate mixture into the cavity of the turkey, make an incision at the neck end of the breast, loosen the skin by making a pocket from breast down to the legs. By using a dessert spoon, fill this pocket with the dressing and close with one or two small skewers the end where the incision has been made.

In the cavity of the turkey place two pounds of chopped apples, one-half pound of fresh butter, chopped nuts and raisins. Add some finely chopped sweet marjoram to the fruit. This blends wonderfully well with the turkey juices and is a most piquant surprise, as is the stuffing which, close to the breast, makes a delicate trimming. The only addition which might pick up the gravy still more is sour cream with a dash of paprika. The stuffing of the cavity is the compote and vegetable for the turkey.

Goose. The goose is marinated like the turkey. The

turkey stuffing is excellent for the goose except that a half pound of calves' liver can be substituted for the goose or chicken liver. The stuffing should be pushed in between the skin and the meat. It should be light, consisting of parsley, sweet marjoram, butter, and mashed potatoes, which absorbs the fat wonderfully, and to this is added the calves' liver. The cavity can be stuffed with chopped apples or sauerkraut, the tartness of which produces an unusual and surprising taste in the meat of the goose, especially if some green dill is available. The sauerkraut, finally removed from the cavity, should be refreshed with a strong dash of ginger ale and served with the goose. When the goose is almost done some potato balls may be added to the pan and when cooked should be served sprinkled with finely chopped chives.

Gosling. Gosling or young goose, which is a broiler, should also have a marinade between skin and meat. For this are recommended parsley, chive, rosemary, chopped spinach leaves, lemon juice and olive oil. When ready to broil there is added to this under-the-skin marinade one-fourth pound of fresh unsalted butter, salt and pepper. The gosling, under a blanket of bacon, should be broiled under a low flame and turned and always basted with some fresh butter. This is a fine roast during the young summer days. Serve with it new potatoes, cottage cheese, *beurre noir* (golden browned butter) and very young green peas.

Duck. The duck (a young one) takes splendidly to an herb marinade mixed with the pulp of an orange. The herbs for the marinade are: Tarragon, rosemary, parsley, chopped onions, garlic, a few caraway seeds, and olive oil. Leave the duck in the marinade in the refrigerator for at least twenty-four hours. Dismiss the marinade if the duck is to be stuffed; otherwise it can stay with the duck in the process of broiling or roasting.

Rescue from the marinade of the duck the rosemary and tarragon; chop them finely (in case dried herbs have been used renew them) and add chopped chervil, parsley and one-half pound unsalted butter. Insert this mixture by the same under-the-skin treatment after salt and pepper have been rubbed in the breast pocket. Place in the cavity of the duck the pulp of one orange. The orange peelings, finely chopped, are steamed for a little while in white wine and set aside for the gravy. The duck, too, has to be roasted in the oven with the prescribed low heat. When the duck is tender, remove the fat from the gravy and prepare the sauce from the juices. Add one tablespoon of flour and a few thin slices of Spanish onion and boil down to a purée. Add the finely chopped orange peeling (without the white underskin) and cook for five minutes and strain. Add one glass of port wine, one tablespoon of brandy, one dash of ginger and a dash of cayenne. Braised celery, red cabbage slowly stewed in wine, small dumplings rolled in parsley, and fresh butter are unique escorts for a young duck.

*Chicken.** A roasting chicken is placed in the following marinade for twelve hours: wild marjoram, onion and parsley, all finely cut if green herbs are used; if dry herbs are used one tablespoon in all, excluding parsley which is always used green, some finely cut shallots, some lemon juice, and one tablespoon of olive oil. If the chicken is to be roasted without stuffing, lard the top with bacon, and give some under-the-skin stuffing of parsley and rosemary, and cook with sour cream in a slow oven. Season inside with salt, pepper, and sweet marjoram.

Capon. Capon is the intimidated yet princely fowl of the chicken family. For its marinading it should be treated with a mixture of juniper berries which have been soaked in white wine for a few hours and with rosemary and bay leaves. The marinade as an under-the-skin treatment remains six hours after which it becomes also the stuffing. Lard the breast and legs and cover with

* For other variations of chicken, see The Demonstrations, Chapter 9.

sour cream. Renew the sour cream after half an hour of baking and finally when the capon is tender, place it for a few minutes under the broiler, covered.

A purée of Jerusalem artichokes (*topinambour*), watercress slightly sprayed with French dressing and a condiment of Apricot-Mostarda, may be company to the capon.

Squab. The French call squab *les poussins.* I became partial to these delicate little birds because when once in a predicament they behaved like gentlemen; they didn't let me down. I had a luncheon for ten friends but the number doubled when friends brought their friends. One day a cavalcade of four automobiles stopped in the lane of my house, on the lake of Thoune in the Bernese Mountains, for one of my "impromptu" luncheons which all my friends very much liked.

Broiled squab were on the original menu but they take time for herb stuffing and treatment. I rushed to the kitchen where my trusted cook stood wringing her hands. On the stove I discovered an enormous kettle with very hot butter. It gave me an idea. I said to my *cordon bleu* that so long as we had ten more squab on hand, they could be thrown into this deep sea of butter. She crossed herself, I stood speechless—no more ideas came—and left the kitchen like a coward. Anything could happen. Somewhat awed I returned after a few minutes, my courage having returned.

"It is a miracle," the cook said, and wiped her brow. And here they were golden brown, oh! so delicate looking, brushed with herb butter and piled like a pyramid on a large round platter with bouquets of fresh herbs and watercress and the lovely bronze lettuce leaves around them. The vegetable with this miracle was a purée of sorrel. It was a happy victory and the fried squab became the rage of all my friends.

The Guinea Hen. The guinea hen belongs to the barnyard now—this exile from the African wilds. The little wild chicken acclimatized itself, only its meat still has somewhat the smoky, strange taste of the wild. Its marinade, which tenderizes the meat, is really the marinade usually placed in game: wild marjoram, juniper berries, Tellicherry pepper, a dash of ginger, garlic, onions, lemon juice and oil. Guinea hen, as with any other game, should never be touched with water, and cleansed only with lemon juice. I know that I cannot convince most cooks not to wash their fowl either, and that lemon is the surest and most sanitary way of cleansing meats. But I hope that from practice the experienced cook will come to the same conclusion. Some cooks let meat soak in water and soak away the finest juices, leaving the meat so insipid that no marinade can replace this loss of quality.

Leave the marinade around the guinea hen. Its little dryness is cured with a blanket of bacon and an under-the-skin treatment with parsley, rosemary, and fresh butter. The low heat, a covering with sour cream, and the treatment are a successful combination—the juniper berry marinade included. The gravy which is very unusual need not be tampered with. It is perfect.

GAME

Game is so rare in many parts of America that it could almost be counted out in the menus of the family. This is a great loss because game has a wonderful quality, thanks to the unbounded freedom of birds and animals in the woods, and their feeding on the finest that grows in nature. All the berries, mushrooms, moss, wild herbs—this is their daily food. They are not slaughtered either; they are shot and fall nobly. There are game laws observed all over the world, but even in game season here, only the very big city markets or the *de luxe* grocery shops carry game. I know that in the Carpathians the peasants would never disturb the game in seasons when it should be left unmolested.

But in this country, with all the woods, mountains, and great isolation, what becomes of all the animals of the woods? Why are most markets empty of them? Those excellent hares (and I don't mean rabbits), the saddles and legs of venison, the pheasants which are worth their weight in gold, or the partridges, and wild duck?

Good game is unforgettable for me, when with the turning of the leaves to golden red, I remember that our hunting lodge in the Carpathian Mountains was opened. Great hunters tried their hands at cooking. Each of them had a specialty in store, and our grandfather whistled happily when his old valet once more tied a big white apron around his waist. Positions were reversed and the cooks tolerantly stood behind the masters, keeping at hand the bottles of sherry, port wine, and the white wine which had to come from the Tyrol (called by us straw wine because the bottles were carefully wrapped in the protective straw of the fields), and red wine from the Hungarian hillsides. Oh, and all the noble essences, herbs, berries—their famous Mostarda and their Rose Hip Marmalade prepared unsweetened especially for game.

When the spits were turning and the ovens were ablaze the hunting lodge was steaming with the fragrance of the woods. It was amazing what exquisite and daring dishes these grand *seigneurs* produced. Grandfather's game birds were tenderly wrapped in grape leaves after being larded with bacon and bathed in brandy which, as was stanchly pretended, combined the illusion of the woods and the vineyards. Later on I learned from the Russian hunters that they also marinated their game, but submerged it in sour cream—they probably preferred to *drink* their brandy—and this one time I thoroughly agreed with the Russians! But all of them were unanimous and laid down as a rule that the humble cabbage of all denominations and colors was the logical vegetable to accompany game. But what disguises they invented, what glamor they lavished on those stubborn cabbages! Chestnuts, walnuts, sweet almonds, prunes, and raisins soaked in wine, and grapes and figs went into the cooking pot. And *choucroute* (plain sauerkraut) was knighted with a strong dash of champagne when elected *aide de camp* to the royal pheasant.

DEER, HARE, AND PHEASANT

This trio, which probably can be bought in the market, were always marinated in my old home with juniper berry, pine needles, mushrooms, onions, garlic, lemon juice, olive oil, and some cumin and wild marjoram in the mixture. Venison was marinated for forty-eight hours, yet deer meat after being shot was immediately treated with a marinade. The meat was sponged with vinegar or lemon juice. The whole carcass was hung up outdoors. The freshly shot pheasant got its marinade inside when still in the feathers because game needs to cool off from the excitement of the chase; little birds like quail should cool off for at least twenty-four hours and partridges even for a few days.

Saddle of Deer or Venison. If venison is bought in the market, soak in marinade for forty-eight hours, lard with bacon cut into narrow strips, dipped in marinade. Rub inside with salt and pepper and dried wild marjoram. Add soaked rose hips*; have oven heat at 250° F. Serve with chestnut purée and currant jelly.

Belgian Hare. Do not confuse hare with rabbit. The hare is an animal of the woods, but mostly lives on young cabbage leaves which it adores, and, to the farmers' distress, prefers the first tender shoots. Hare meat is delicate; it is hidden beneath a rather tough top skin which, with a sharp thin knife, can be removed like a glove. After skinning the hare, cut it in two parts. The saddle with the hind legs is for roasting, broiling, or

* Rose hips are available, dried, from wholesale herb houses. Fine grocers will order them on request.

braising. All of the other parts make that famous *ragoût*, "*civet de lièvre.*"

The marinade for a saddle of hare is one teaspoon juniper berries, ground, one-half teaspoon wild marjoram, three shallots, peel of one lemon, juice of half a lemon, and two tablespoons of olive oil. Marinate for twenty-four hours. The saddle and hind legs not separated are generously larded with bacon in strips. Rub inside with lemon juice and salt and pepper. Add some of the marinade, then place in baking pan. Cover with sour cream, and bake in a 250° F. oven approximately one and one-half hours. While hare is baking cook soaked rose hips in their red wine and, when soft, strain through cheesecloth. Before serving add rose hips to the gravy. It forms a delicate sauce with bacon, sour cream, and the juices of the hare. Serve with noodles or wild rice and red cabbage.

Ragoût of Hare ("*Civet de Lièvre*"). Cut half a pound of bacon in small squares. Place in a deep casserole and soften bacon in the heat of the oven. Add one large onion cut in thin slices, two carrots and one turnip cut in small pieces, two crushed bay leaves, one sprig of thyme and rosemary, and two glasses of red wine. Stew *ragoût* (front legs, breast, and giblets). After thirty minutes add another glass of wine. Tightly cover and cook in a low oven until tender. Season with salt and pepper, half a teaspoon of brown sugar, and a dash of cayenne. Remove sprigs of herbs; smooth sauce with two tablespoons of sour cream.

Partridge à la Newsky. Split partridge down the backbone. Rub inside with lemon juice and ground juniper berries. Salt mildly. Tie partridge in bacon strips, and if possible into grape leaves. Cook in a slow oven. Pour three tablespoons sour cream over the partridge. Before serving add one and one-half ounces herb butter (rosemary, basil, and chervil).

Bohemian Pheasant. Pheasants bought in the market are usually cool enough to be prepared for cooking. Never touch pheasant with water. Rub inside and outside with lemon juice and marinate for twenty-four hours. For this use one tablespoon juniper berries, ground, one-half teaspoon wild marjoram (dried), two shallots, parsley, two tablespoons olive oil, and one-half tablespoon lemon juice. Cover larded pheasant with grape leaves. If grape leaves are not available, use leaves of savoy cabbage. Season inside with salt and paprika. Place in baking pan with sour cream and a glass of red wine, and bake in a slow oven, 250° F. Before serving add one glass of sherry. Serve with sauerkraut which can be improved with a dash of ginger ale.

CHAPTER SEVEN

Fish and Crustaceans

WHEN I THINK OF FISH I think of wide streams; I think of mountain brooks, of great languid lakes—calm on their surface but tumultuous in their depth, of small lakes upon which one comes with surprise on high plains or in the high Alps between rocks like deep, gray unfathomable eyes. And I never thought that fish could be eaten otherwise than immediately after being caught, or sent in fresh-water tanks by rapid trains, or kept alive in the depths of boats by letting the water circulate through small holes in the tanks.

In Switzerland we went fishing high up where the ferns ended and the waterfalls started. Our guides on such excursions had especially long containers filled with water into which the lively trout were thrown and carried on long poles down to the village. There these containers were let into the village rivulet, the long tanks chained to the poles of a narrow bridge. From these tanks every day our cook would fish her trout for dinner.

Thus fish eating was romantic and the fish freshness had to be preserved under all conditions. Once on an exploring automobile ride on the mountain road between Interlaken and Thoune, we were stopping at an old château which had been turned into an exclusive dining place. The approach to the old manor house was superb —through a long alley of wonderful old chestnut trees, the tops forming a canopy through which a silvery moon was gleaming. At the end stood the old gray château, solemn and silent, untouched for centuries. It was early summer, but because the evenings in such altitude were always cool, woodfires were blazing in the big hall through which we had to pass to come to the terraced garden dining rooms in the rear. In a rondel was a naturally caught fountain, the waters spouting high up and gathering in an eternal play at a vast stone basin. All was fantastically beautiful and the privacy of the guest tables was protected by rocks and stone curves like screens. It was an amusing surprise when, after having chosen a "blue" trout, we were invited to select the size from the stone basin around the fountain. There happy little well-fed trout were lustily diving and jumping and evading the net in which they were eventually caught, to become the "blue" trout.

Fish are most congenial to herb treatment, especially trout, as in the "blue" dish.

BLUE SPECKLED TROUT

This is one of the delicacies which is most surprising. The secret of the success of this dish is the absolute freshness of the trout. The trout and carp—perhaps the shad, too—are of the fine-scaled fish which keep a jelly-like substance around their scales. Therefore if one intends to cook them the "blue" way the fish has to come right from the water, be killed rapidly, and cleaned without injuring the skin. This kind of fish, taken from the water, should neither be washed nor scaled.

A bouillon of carrots, onions, parsley, and celery should be simmered slowly, the vegetables cooked to pieces, salted to taste, strained, a dash of basil and thyme added, and the bouillon returned to the casserole and brought to active boiling; the trout, before being placed in the boiling bouillon, receives a dash of boiling vinegar which, combined with the hot bouillon, immediately turns the trout this fantastic blue color. It is a very decorative fish, served with herb butter (chervil and chive), watercress, and new small parsley potatoes.

CARP BLUE

In Europe, carp is considered one of the most delicious fish, and Christmas Eve, or Christmas Day, dinners are almost inconceivable without it. It is the mirror carp which lends itself to this preparation. It is treated exactly as the blue speckled trout, except that the carp needs double time for cooking in its vegetable broth. It is served with freshly grated horseradish, mixed with whipped cream (unsweetened).

FRIED CARP

The carp is scaled, cut in one and one-half inch slices, left for one hour in a light marinade of lemon juice, a few finely cut shallots, parsley, tarragon, and a dash of olive oil. From the marinade which is brushed off lightly the carp is rolled first in salted flour, dipped in egg yolk beaten with a tablespoon of water, then rolled again in fine bread crumbs, which are pressed tightly around the fish.

The best frying mixture for fish is oil mixed with precooked butter. (See page 191.) The frying kettle should be deep and spacious so that the fish can be submerged. When turned to a golden brown the fish is placed on blotting paper or paper toweling and served on a very hot platter. Parsley sprigs are likewise dipped in flour and the beaten egg and thrown into the sizzling frying fat, and when crisp top the carp. Celery-root salad is always very good served with fried carp.

SOLE À LA MARINA (FILLET OF FLOUNDER)

For four people two pounds of fillets of flounder are necessary. Two ounces of fresh butter are mixed with one-half of a finely chopped Bermuda onion. This is stewed in one-half glass of white wine until the onions are very soft. One-half pound of mushrooms are cut in slices not too thin, and added. The fish, seasoned with salt and paprika, should be cooked in this five minutes; then finely chopped tarragon, basil and chervil (one tablespoon; one-half teaspoon if dried), one-half glass of white wine in which one-fourth teaspoon of potato flour has been diluted, are added while sauce is boiling, and cooked for two more minutes. The yolks of two eggs are beaten with one-half teaspoon of lemon juice, then a dash of cayenne is added. The sole is removed to a very hot platter, the thick sauce poured over it, lobster butter placed on top, and the whole returned to a hot oven for five minutes.

BAKED PIKE

Into the baking dish go two ounces of butter, one Bermuda onion cut in slices, three slices of bacon cut to small squares, one-half teaspoon of paprika, and three tablespoons of sour cream. The pike is baked in a 300° F. oven, and basted frequently with sour cream. The fish must not be allowed to get dry; when done it is placed in a baking dish and herb butter placed on top and allowed to melt. Potatoes cut in thin round slices can be baked with the fish.

SALMON ROYAL

The salmon should be cleaned with lemon juice after it is scaled—inside and outside. If the salmon is used whole, herb butter in any kind of herb combination can be placed inside. If it is used in one-inch thick slices or thicker they also are rubbed with lemon juice first, then salted and peppered with Sarawak pepper.

To boil the salmon one has to prepare (for four slices of salmon) one finely cut Bermuda onion which is placed in a saucepan with one-half cup of white wine and cooked until onions are very tender, the whole forming a purée-like substance. Bed the salmon slices on this purée, add four more tablespoons of white wine, cover and let steam in oven for fifteen minutes. The sauce can be used with the salmon with one tablespoon of heavy cream added, and seasoned with one tablespoon of finely chopped green dill, or, if not available, tarragon is just as effective. The salmon also can be used without the sauce and served with a Hollandaise sauce seasoned with tarragon. If served with the wine sauce in which the salmon has been prepared, freshly grated horseradish mixed with lemon juice is exceedingly good.

SHRIMPS WITH DILL SAUCE

The shrimps are washed thoroughly in several waters before being used. One-half teaspoon summer savory, onions, and some leeks are added to the water in which they are boiled; the water is set aside for further use. Shell the boiled shrimps, remove the dark vein, and add a fine white sauce of two tablespoons butter and one tablespoon of flour, blended thoroughly to a fine yellow, thinned with shrimp bouillon and seasoned with salt and white pepper. Two tablespoons of finely chopped green dill and two tablespoons of heavy cream are added, and the shrimps placed in the sauce and heated a moment. The shrimps are served in patty shells or in a rim of boiled rice mixed with fresh green peas cooked separately.

BOUILLABAISSE AMÉRICAINE

This is the American version of the famous *Bouillabaisse Marseillaise.* With excellent fish in abundance one should come pretty close to creating a worthwhile substitute. Fish of southern waters are preferable and the variety of five different kinds of fish which go with *bouillabaisse* can be selected from among the following seven: red snapper, pompano, mullet, bass, mackerel, and pike. Lobster, of course, is a delicious addition to this dish. For six helpings, three pounds of fish and one and one-half pounds of lobster are necessary. The heads, tails, and backbones of fish to be used in the *bouillabaisse* are cooked for one hour in water with parsley roots, one-half teaspoon of origanum (wild marjoram), two cloves of garlic, and one-fourth teaspoon of fine spices. After an hour, the lobster goes into the above bouillon. Shallots cut in fine rings and finely chopped parsley (one teaspoon) are sautéed in oil, the fish, cut in generous pieces, added, covered with strained fish bouillon and cooked very slowly. Seasonings of salt, paprika, and a pinch of saffron are added. Six slices of white bread are toasted, brushed with oil, rubbed with garlic, and sprinkled with chopped chives. Fish and bouillon are served in individual soup plates, with a slice of toast on top, then the lobster placed on top of the bread. *Bouillabaisse* also can be served from an oval tureen, with bread and lobster on top.

CÔTELETTES OF SWORDFISH AUX FINES HERBES

Côtelettes (or cutlets) of swordfish are sprinkled with salt and paprika, rolled in flour, and sautéed in fresh butter. When *côtelettes* are turned, finely chopped shallots, parsley, chervil, tarragon, and mushrooms, two tablespoons in all, a teaspoon of lemon juice, and one-half glass of white wine are added, and the whole cooked five minutes longer.

CÔTELETTES OF SALMON

The salmon cutlets are salted, rolled in flour, and placed in a very hot skillet with plenty of butter. Finely chopped capers, tarragon, parsley, and one-half teaspoon of lemon juice are added. Seasonings are paprika and a dash of cayenne.

CURRY LOBSTER

The water in which the lobster is boiled is prepared as follows: one teaspoon caraway seed, a bunch of Italian parsley with root, one bunch of leeks cut in strips, and one-half teaspoon of salt added. All are boiled for twenty minutes. Then the well-brushed lobster is added with the water boiling *very actively*. The water must remain vigorously boiling until the lobster is red and done. Then it is cut in two and topped with butter of fine herbs (basil, chervil, tarragon, and chive finely chopped). Curry sauce thinned with the lobster bouillon is served.

LOBSTER CROQUETTES

The lobster meat is chopped fine, and herb butter the size of a big walnut and one slice of white bread soaked in cream are added. This is seasoned with salt and white pepper, and mixed thoroughly. After shaping, the croquettes are rolled first in flour, then in beaten egg, and last in bread crumbs, and fried in *deep* hot butter. Green peas or asparagus tips may be served with these croquettes. (Canned lobster may be used the same way, after being drained.)

LOBSTER EN COQUILLE

Boiled lobster meat is cut in small pieces, then finely cut mushrooms sautéed in sour cream, and finely chopped parsley and chives are added. Salt and paprika season the mixture, which is then placed in oven-proof shells, sprinkled with Parmesan cheese and sour cream, topped with lobster butter, and placed under the broiler for ten minutes. (See lobster butter, page 167.)

OYSTERS

Freshly opened oysters left on the half shell can be served with cold horseradish sauce (made of freshly grated horseradish). Abroad, especially in England, cheese in small squares is served with oysters.

OYSTERS BROILED

Freshly opened oysters on the half shell are sprinkled with finest olive oil, a few drops of lemon juice, a dash of white pepper, and topped with sweet butter mixed with finely chopped parsley, then broiled quickly (an after-theater dish).

OYSTER STEW BORDEAUX

Two ounces of anchovy butter are melted, and one tablespoon of finely chopped parsley, a pinch of garlic, one glass of red wine, and fifteen oysters fresh from the shell with their juice are added. Bread crumbs fried in olive oil are sprinkled on top, then all placed in a very hot oven, covered with paper, and brought to the boiling point. (Unsalted butter must be used when mixing with anchovies.)

OYSTER RAGOÛT—SALPICON GOURMET

Twenty freshly opened oysters are heated in one pint of white wine and one teaspoon of lemon juice, rapidly. The oysters are removed and set aside. The juice, and white sauce made of sweet butter, are added, and boiled down until very thick. One tablespoon of lobster butter, the yolks of two eggs, five mushrooms cut in slices, one piece of truffle cut finely (canned), ten shrimps, freshly cooked, smoked tongue cut in small squares, and one anchovy are then added; then the oysters. All is mixed well by covering the casserole and shaking it, then seasoned carefully with salt, a dash of cayenne, and one teaspoon finely chopped tarragon. This is placed in *coquilles* (shells), and sprinkled with bread crumbs and lobster butter, then the shells placed on a large pan and broiled under a strong heat for a few minutes. This *ragoût,* called *Salpicon Gourmet,* is exquisite for cold buffets or as an entrée for a sumptuous dinner or luncheon.

CHAPTER EIGHT

Making Menus and Some Special Soups

MENUS HAVE TO BE DEMONSTRATED—actually rehearsed, retouched, judged—before they should go before the credulous and trusting family and guests, especially because of the herbs, the use of which is still remote to the average cook. I love herbs and I thoroughly understand their mission in the *cuisine.* After having written my first chapters explaining herbs and explaining myself and my relation to herbs in my own plans, I suddenly arrived at a stopping place. After having analyzed the use of herbs in general I objected to writing recipes. These formulas on paper do not show at all what I wish to give and make plastically clear. It is impossible for one's imagination, however flourishing, to understand how "sweet marjoram" or "basil," or fine or robust herbs, will make a good and sober dish perfect.

Therefore some demonstrations were planned, and through the practical experience in the presence of my "pupils" I began to see my way clear and unobstructed.

It was a joy and a revelation, and I am greatly rewarded by the keen understanding of this circle of young Americans, all of them ambitious to remodel their recipes. Herbs have become for them, from a strange and somewhat misunderstood fad, an everyday necessity in their food. And not only the inexperienced ones but those who are highly recognized hostesses follow these new interpretations of foods, my principles and basic reasons for balancing menus. It is my aim to simplify the menu, to slenderize it while making meals fascinating.

The planning of the daily meals cannot be negligently done. It is a very serious task when it concerns the family. Our dinners should not only be the finest expression of our material life but they should create contentment and joy and satisfaction within the family—the meal itself and its consequences. The word "menu" is loosely used; it needs stabilization; it needs definite rules upon which to rest. In former times there were seasons for certain foods which made the rule, and it was not superstition but wisdom which made it so. There were winter menus and foods; menus for the spring differently dosed, as the French people express it: *légumes chauffants et légumes rafraîchissants,* heating or cooling vegetables. There were menus decidedly for the summer, and opulent autumn menus for the time when the harvest, the wonderful restfulness of ripeness, comes over nature and mankind.

This all has gone out of style. We eat forced strawberries in the middle of winter because they have become a great source of income for the southern states, transportation no longer being an obstacle. Mankind has grown almost hectically impatient—his hurry has become part of his way of living. There are no longer the exciting *primeurs,* things new and first in the market. The American market is still a wonder to me and yet it does not create the joyful feeling that I have had in "natural" markets of having seen the first asparagus, which meant spring was in full swing and the summer close at hand. It is a great study—what to do with all this abundance about us without being crushed by it.

What is the rule which is comprehensive enough to be standardized? I would nominate the soup as a fixture, one thing so amazingly old—that was, that is, that will be. After the importance of bread, comes the soup—the one beginning to the main meal—soup desired, soup expected, soup exhilarating, satisfying, pacifying—soup for the hunger of the family. Indeed it must be the soup which in my planning is going to tyrannize the menu. And I discovered that as long as people have eaten soup, there have always been three kinds of soup:

A. The bouillon,
B. The creamed soup,
C. The purée soup.

THE BOUILLON (CONSOMMÉ)

The bouillon is the essence of meat, poultry, fish, game, crustaceans. These are a never-ending source of the bouillons, yet very little is known of the great variety of vegetable bouillons. All bouillons are clear, slender, and exhilarating, like precious old wine. They are served in small cups. It is the bouillon which enlivens the appetite, animates the tired mind and body. And the menu around the bouillon can be expansive and rich in calories.

THE CREAMED SOUP (POTAGE)

Oh! this one makes use of everything the bouillon consists of and in addition builds itself up on material that mostly is ignorantly discarded and thrown out. Yes, the cream soup is basically a product of vegetable water or of the light bouillons in which meat and poultry and fish have been boiled for their own sake, without any regard for further use; these fine waters which on the sly capture a great many of the vitamins, still have the delicate perfume and aromas of the foods, and with the help of egg yolks and cream become the beloved velvety soup. Combinations of cream soups are very fascinating—and their variety can be made without limit. With all the good things that are smuggled into the cream soup, still it is the herbal contribution which finally makes its goodness interesting.

Herbs in cream soup are as alluring as the jewels in the attire of an elegant woman. Indeed the cream soup is a warm feminine soup and every trick is permissible for touching it up. Cream soups have the most pacifying influence upon the hungry family. Yet never forget there must follow a finely balanced, sober but light, menu with the accent on the green salads or vegetables, which make variety in the menu. In such a menu meats or poultry should be broiled, or braised, their natural juices respected, heightened only by seasonings with herbs or spices and sometimes by the fine aroma of wine.

The dessert will be quite a problem because eggs and cream have been used already in the soup and should not be repeated. In old Austria they had a way out of completing such a menu charmingly: the dessert was right on the table from the beginning of the meal—dessert and table decoration in one. It was called *giardinetto* (little garden) and all that is good was piled on the old-fashioned fruit bowl. All kinds of fruit—side by side with pears, apples, plums, and grapes were dates or raisins and figs, almonds and nuts, alluring little cakes and for the more serious minded in appetite there were little cheeses in colored paper. Unforgettable these *giardinetti,* the everlasting surprise and joy of the youth in the family.

THE PURÉE SOUP

The purée soup is essence and vegetable in one and stands absolutely on its own. It is the grand soup *par excellence* with all its lentils, beans, and peas of all denominations as the basic material—and possibly cereals and potatoes and all the fresh vegetables included. What an abundance of vitamins and calories, and so little used in the daily menu! Herbs are indispensable in these soups and excellent company for their heartiness. Purée soups refuse to be burdened with additional flour. They are entirely independent of this because of their faculty for thickening and thinning soups. It is *the* soup for little growing children, for students and athletes, and especially for all who are intelligently active. Of course the menu which is in the wake of such a soup must be extremely slender—something with Lent in mind, the atoning of our sins.

And now I feel that our appetite is greatly aroused and curiosity stimulated for getting acquainted with some of the examples of the different varieties of those soups which have become the managing factor of the daily menu.

BOUILLONS

And while the readers might expect to see all the familiar bouillons of chicken and meats re-explained, I skip all of those because the cook is very well acquainted with them and by now she knows the delicate addition of sprinkling herbs on top of these bouillons or adding herbs while in the process of cooking. I am anxious to introduce the essence of vegetables as bouillon: their stabilizing position in the making of menus.

Mushroom Bouillon. When I first presented the mushroom bouillon to my pupils they were amazed that such a culinary wonder could be of such infinite simplicity in its make-up. Culinary wonder? I studied the compositions of my old formulas for soups—they consisted mostly of ten to fifteen different ingredients. But these ingredients and their influence were explained in their relation to the foundation of the mushroom soup, and this was enlightening. Thus I found the first part of the recipe for an ideal mushroom bouillon based upon the wonderfully aromatic and substantial stone mushroom which gave the soup its quality. The stone mushroom is a mushroom growing wild all over the European country in oak woods and it grows from June to October, especially when the weather is damp. What would the French do without their *cèpe,* the Russians without their *griboui,* and the Austrians without their *steinpilze?* It is a great delicacy—I prefer it to truffles—and it grows for poor and rich alike.

In America I had to satisfy myself with the cultivated field mushroom, a very solid, white, and lovely mushroom. Its aroma asserted itself in my bouillon splendidly. Only the humblest part of the mushroom is used. I took one pound of mushrooms for four people. I want to emphasize that one must never wash the mushrooms. The mushroom is a damp soil product and attracts water and when soaked its fine juices become watered. Wipe off earth. Peel the mushroom, cap and stems; set aside the caps. The peelings and the stems undergo a rapid showerbath to free them from the light sands in which they grew. The peelings and stems from one pound go into a pot with two quarts of water. Add to the mushrooms one tablespoon of caraway seed and one sweet onion (Spanish or Bermuda). Don't salt until the bouillon is strained. Let the bouillon cook slowly one hour. Set it aside to settle several hours for the assimilation of mushrooms, onion, and caraway seed. I like to make this bouillon a day ahead and then I get perfect results.

In the meantime the caps have been sprinkled with lemon juice so as not to lose their whiteness. As soon as the mushroom bouillon is placed again on the range, grate eight of the mushroom caps. At the second part of the boiling of the bouillon add one sprig of dried or fresh wild marjoram. After half an hour the bouillon will be reduced to half the amount. Season with two teaspoons (level) of coarse salt and one-half teaspoon of black pepper freshly grated. Put the bouillon through a fine strainer, press the exhausted stems, peelings, onion, and even the seeds through the strainer so that not one drop of the fine essence shall be lost. Place the grated caps either in the tureen or in the individual bouillon cups and pour in the hot bouillon. Add croutons of black bread spread with unsalted herb butter. Fresh chive butter is good.

Lentil Bouillon. Lentils have established themselves immediately among my friends and pupils and again it is the fine simplicity, the lentil essence pure and undisturbed which is most popular. Two cups of lentils for four people. (I prefer the little brown lentil, the Russian kind.) Wash the lentils thoroughly and soak overnight in a bowl with enough water to cover. To this water add one quart of water when the lentils are placed in the cooking pot—two quarts, in all, of cold water, starting on a low fire. The lentils will expand in slowly boiling water (uncovered). Add one bouquet of thyme and green fennel (if dry, one teaspoon of fennel seed is used), and two teaspoons of coarse salt. When after one hour the lentils are soft and the water reduced to the amount needed, the essence will already be strong. Strain the bouillon—avoid puréeing the lentils, which when cold still make a delicious salad. Add to the lentil bouillon for each cup a few drops of Maggi sauce, which is a very old extract of vegetable made in Switzerland where herbs and vegetables are of a special goodness and strength. Serve with tiny hot biscuits stuffed with some fragrant herb butter mixture. When hot, lentil bouillon may be poured over one tablespoon finely scraped raw beef (round steak); this is recommended for an invalid diet.

Spinach Bouillon. Nothing is more delicious for bouillon than the water in which spinach has been cooked. I found out that spinach too can be made into a bouillon without being creamed. One pound for each person is needed to bring out the essence, and the joy that one pound of spinach can give is amazing. It is one of the year-round vegetables always in the market. The beginning of this recipe is the usual one. The spinach has to have many showers until the fine sands which creep into all tiny crevices of the leaves are swept away. Take hot water first and then gradually cold water so that the spinach is its crispy self when finally placed in the cooking pot. The pot should contain double the amount of cold water that is needed. Bring the spinach slowly to the boiling point; give the spinach time to develop its excellent juices. After half an hour of boiling add one sprig of origanum (wild marjoram), which gives the bouillon an intriguing aroma. Let it boil for another half hour. Set the spinach bouillon aside and let it slowly cool down, which helps the first assimilation. (It is advisable to cook spinach in an enamel pot.)

Give the spinach another hour to cook (it might be the next day even) and when this last stage is reached drain the spinach; press the leaves so as to get the entire essence into the bouillon. The leaves will be totally spent and should be discarded. They have done their work! It is this very slow cooking which prevents the spinach from developing the somewhat astringent taste.

Add to the bouillon the seasoning: half a teaspoon of coarse salt, one teaspoon of fresh marjoram, a teaspoon of lemon juice, and a teaspoon of Savita, an American vegetable extract. One hard-boiled egg minced finely can be placed in four cups and the hot bouillon poured over it. Grated Parmesan cheese added is excellent.

Asparagus Bouillon. While most of us love asparagus taken from the steaming kettle, we leave the most interesting part of the vegetable behind. Or it may be made into a thick cream sauce. This does not quite do justice to the amazing fineness of the asparagus bouillon—another possibility. Set the tops of one pound of asparagus aside, cut the other part to small bits (discard the woody part), and place them in two quarts of cold water. As soon as it starts boiling add two leeks (white part only) cut in small pieces, and let this cook slowly until the soup water is reduced to one quart and the asparagus and leeks are completely exhausted. The bouillon then will be of a fine green, thanks to the sprig of borage which is added after an hour's cooking. Strain, and again press down the material, and strain to the last drop. Season with coarse salt and return to the pot. Bring the bouillon to the boiling point; add the heads of the asparagus which are done in a short time, adding a fresh zesty taste. They must be firm when served. Place in the cups herb butter—finely minced tarragon or dried tarragon mixed with minced parsley. Pour the hot bouillon over this.

Beet Bouillon. This is the very delicate offspring of the Russian *borsht.* Made without meat, its whole value is extracted from the beet itself with the help of caraway seeds, shallots or Bermuda onion, and herbs, topped with sour cream. It needs three beets per person to obtain the strength of the essence. The beets unpeeled but thoroughly scrubbed are put into water, double the amount of which will be needed. Add caraway seeds, one-fourth teaspoon per person, half a shallot (or Bermuda onion) finely minced; add a few drops of herb vinegar. Let boil until beets are tender, remove from the water, peel and return to the liquid two of the three beets. Set aside the third one. The bouillon should continue to boil until beets fall to pieces entirely drained of their juices. Strain through a fine sieve and try to obtain all that is left in the beets. Add the salt needed, a few drops of lemon juice, and a dash of sugar. The other beet is grated and placed with a *soupçon* of finely chopped green dill in the cup or soup plate. The hot bouillon is poured over it and topped with sour cream (sweet heavy cream also is delicious). This soup can be served hot, or cold in summer (the preparation is the same).

These are a few samples of the possibilities of fresh vegetable bouillons. And around these sober, most appetizing bouillons the menus can be built in great variety. The bouillon is indeed the leading spirit which takes from the menu its uniformity because there is a limited variety to the meat and fowl dishes. Today menus really have narrowed down to a few conventional dishes, even though herbs bring great possibility of flavoring to these.

CREAMED SOUPS

Creamed soups are well-known and I will not disturb the cooks who probably have standard recipes for their favorites in this group. If they will top each serving with some finely cut green herbs, the soups will gain in flavor and looks. I wish they would abstain from the heavy *coulis*—too much flour in too little butter—and use cream beaten with egg yolks (well seasoned) instead. While beating add a few spoonfuls of the hot soup with a few drops of lemon juice (never boil the cream); then pour the hot soup over the beaten eggs and cream. It is a foaming soup and a very light and velvety one.

Cream of Cucumber. A light and aromatic stock is first prepared for the cream of cucumber: one calf's foot, one Bermuda onion, two carrots, one turnip, and a sprig of thyme. When calf's foot and vegetables have cooked themselves to pieces in two quarts of water and have been reduced to one quart of bouillon, strain, season with salt, and set aside.

For the cream of cucumber, one small, unpeeled cucumber for each person is cut into thin slices. One pint of cream is added, and the cucumbers cooked on a low fire until the substance gets creamy and thickens, and the cucumbers have spent all their juices. One tablespoon of grated Bermuda onion is added shortly before straining. After being strained and returned to the saucepan for a few minutes, finely chopped chervil, parsley, and chive, two tablespoons in all, are added to the hot cucumber soup. Before it is served either in tureen or individually, a dash of lemon juice, a tablespoon of cucumber cream and a teaspoon of sour cream are placed in tureen or cup, and finally the calf's-foot stock is added. If this soup is served cold it has to be placed in the refrigerator for three hours. Small rye-krisps spread with chive butter are delicious with cream of cucumber soup.

A simplified version of cucumber soup for summer, to be eaten cold, omitting all meat stock, can be made as follows: one cup of barley washed and then soaked for several hours. Using the same water with an additional quart of fresh water, boil slowly until barley is very soft. Strain, season with salt, pepper, and lemon juice. Use this instead of meat stock in the above cucumber soup.

Cream of Sorrel. Sorrel is one of those neglected delicate summer vegetables which can be used in great variety. Any kind of stock for soups (meat, chicken, or vegetable, spinach preferred) will lend itself for a cream of sorrel soup. Sorrel grows wild in the fields and probably is available in Italian market places. The sorrel has to be scalded with hot water, then cut in strips and chopped finely. Fresh butter is heated in a pan, the sorrel added and cooked in the butter (covered) for fifteen minutes. Then half a tablespoon of flour is dissolved in a little bouillon or vegetable stock and added to butter and sorrel, lightly thickened; then mixed with stock and cooked for a few minutes. Seasoned with salt and white pepper, finely chopped chive and parsley, it is poured into cups into which one teaspoon of heavy cream mixed with a few drops of lemon juice has been placed. This is a very refreshing soup to be used warm or cold.

THE PURÉE

The puréed soup presents after all only the problem of preferred thickness. The borages, summer and winter savories, wild marjoram, parsley, and the leaves of the celery root are the addition for these congenial *légumes.*

Potato Soup. I like to call the following recipe, "Potato Soup, from a Hungarian *Puszta.*" It was a warm summer day in the Carpathian foothills, the fields in golden ripeness, acacia woods in bloom, a mischievous gravel road and an obstinate automobile that stifled, and decidedly objected to our exploring spirit.

Utterly stranded at sundown, we were finally loaded on an empty hay wagon by a charitable young peasant who had spied our monster from the fields.

Jostled over a bumpy strip of country road between undulating seas of green oats, we approached an alley of silvery birch trees. We had come upon a *puszta.* A Hungarian ranch, or *puszta,* has to be discovered; no one could ever come upon it by means of a straight highway. And here was the low-spreading, friendly, red-roofed house. The young peasant most chivalrously bowed from the hips and opened the door wide for us to enter.

Around their dinner table, covered with gay earthen

plates and bowls, sat the picturesque Hungarian peasant family. When I tried haltingly to apologize they laughed gaily and gave no signs of curiosity or surprise. Instead they quickly made room for us at their table. There were plates and spoons for us, and promising wine glasses, too.

Oh, this amazing soup! Our plates were filled and refilled, to the great joy of our round and graceful hostess. I got the recipe of this bewitching soup, and again I discovered that there is no great difference between the taste of the peasant and the *blasé* taste of the gourmet. On the *puszta* herbs grew in profusion. Tarragon or sweet marjoram was not a fetish to them.

Here is the recipe from this unforgettable peaceful *puszta:*

Two pounds of potatoes, the mealy kind, unpeeled, go into two quarts of water, and some caraway seeds (two tablespoons) with one teaspoon of coarse salt added. After half an hour the potatoes are taken from the water, peeled, cut in small pieces, and returned to the water. Six leeks are cut into small pieces—the white part only; the green pieces are added in their whole length. After another half hour, the green pieces of the leeks are removed and the soup boiled down, potatoes and leeks to a soft purée. When strained it is returned to the pot, one quart of whole milk is added, and two teaspoons of fresh (or dried) marjoram, one teaspoon of coarse salt, and one teaspoon of paprika. The whole is cooked fifteen minutes longer. Warm or cold it is one of those superbly refreshing soups. Before serving, heavy cream and two tablespoons of finely cut parsley are added, and more salt, if needed.

CHAPTER NINE

The Demonstrations

WHERE THERE ARE DEMONSTRATIONS, as with my American pupils, there must be a definite rule to follow in order to make these demonstrations workable. This is a very difficult task because new ideas sometimes will run away with the cook in the midst of some lesson. If cooking is an art, it is a very tricky art, and a dish really never is finished, even if the recipe or formula is strictly followed. Too much depends upon the personal touch. Yet one has to be extremely careful about this personal touch. There should be left a certain freedom to change dishes to one's own liking; and with this idea in mind I made the basic rule of a dish definite, while being not too catholic about variations to achieve new flavors.

My first demonstration was staged in the house of the collaborating editor of this book. She is a woman of high ability and in any undertaking has the great gift of always coöperating fully. Her charming house was turned over entirely and most interestingly to this presentation of "the herbs." It became a house of herbs—of herb sprays, of herb bouquets in vases, of bowls of the herbal salads, symphonies in green, and a showing of all the herbal world which was not only exhibited but used.

The conservatory, a small enclosed porch, was the place of our first activities. Here the fine herbs were exhibited as little plants, and the robust herbs as stately opulent sprays, while dried herbs were arranged in a row of neatly labeled jars—substituting for the fine herbs after their outdoor life was over. With wooden bowls, scissors, and chopping knives at hand the first lesson began by showing how the fine herbs have to be cut for the various preparations which appeared on the first menu. In the center of the display of little herb plants, very noticeable, stood our liaison herb, the chive —very green, erect, and quite aristocratic looking.

First came the mixing for the herb butter—the knowledge of which is the *a b c* of the herbal *cuisine:* parsley, chive, and chervil in butter is a combination which makes excellent sandwiches. The second demonstration was the cutting of herbs for salad; rosemary, burnet, and tarragon still green, the last sprigs of the late fall, were used. Then the sweet marjoram was introduced as the mainstay for the herb mixture of an herb omelet, or an omelet of fine herbs. The supporting herbs were a mixture of dried herbs, which I have called omelet herbs. After the herbs for the three different uses were explained and actually cut and mixed by the hands of this group of pupils, we moved to the kitchen.

There the herbs cut for the sandwiches were mixed with butter (butter unsalted and of the freshest—which I immediately and definitely established as rule A for the herbal *cuisine*). The most alluring herb butter was spread on very thin slices of dark bread—an irresistible combination. We liked the Russian pumpernickel, but any whole wheat or rye bread is good for this. Then came the great moment of the menu—the omelet of fine herbs. I demonstrated three omelets and then turned over instruments and pans to the class, also three different mixtures of herbs for them to choose from. After a short time they came into the dining room triumphantly exhibiting their first omelets of fine herbs.

At the table in front of me was the big salad bowl, with the crisp lettuce, the cress, and the diced cucumber in a side bowl. Neatly arranged on a tray were oil, vinegar, lemon, salt and pepper, the fresh rosemary, burnet, tarragon and chives, the dried herbal mixture and one clove of garlic cut in slices. They thoroughly enjoyed my salad making (described on page 74). The little herbs triumphed in the luncheon of course; their flavors added to this simple menu an extraordinary zest and after this first attempt the group left, enchanted with their discoveries and loaded down with new herbal expressions, with little herbal bouquets and little jars of dried herbs. This was the beginning of a series of demonstrations, each of which proved anew the great value, variety, and novelty of herbs in foods.

THE FIRST MENU

Mushroom bouillon
Sandwiches spread with herbal butter
Omelet of fine herbs
Salad of three greens, the French dressing
plus herbs
Demi-tasse

The mushroom bouillon (see page 144) was brought to this demonstration half finished because such a bouillon needs time to mellow. The pupils received the exact recipe as given in Chapter 8, under "Bouillons."

This first luncheon menu was entirely devoted to the easiest ways of introducing herbs. But the combination contained sufficient nutritive value: the sober soup, the sandwiches rich in calories and vitamins, the omelet of eggs, and the salad of greens with a dressing rich in the finest oils. One easily can enlarge on such a menu by adding cheese to serve with the salad, or a dessert of some kind of pudding. Then this same menu might just as well become a dinner. Individual omelets, besides using herbs, can be filled with cooked chopped ham or calf's brain. Or the salad can be served with cold meats. These are only a few of the possibilities.

THE SECOND MENU

Lentil bouillon
Tiny hot biscuits with herbal stuffing
Chicken livers *en brochette*
Celery-root salad
Demi-tasse

The lentil bouillon was explained in Chapter 8. The biscuits served were the usual hot baking-powder variety. Broken in two, they were stuffed with an herbal mixture made of a few leaves of spinach (raw and finely chopped), chive and chervil, green and refreshing, and fresh butter; salt and pepper and a few drops of lemon juice were added.

Chicken livers *en brochette* is an attractive dish. For six people, use one pound of chicken livers, one-fourth pound of bacon and twelve mushrooms. Have six skewers five inches long. Put chicken livers in a marinade for three hours. For this, use one sprig of thyme, two crushed bay leaves, three minced shallots, one-half clove of garlic cut in slices, one tablespoon of olive oil, one teaspoon of lemon juice, one-fourth teaspoon freshly ground pepper. Mix the marinade well in a bowl and roll the chicken livers in the mixture (do not salt). Cut bacon in one-inch squares. Use the caps of the mushrooms. Peel them (do not wash). Sprinkle with lemon juice. Before removing the livers from the marinade have the oven heated to 400° F. Brush off the marinade before spearing on skewers, alternating: liver, bacon, mushroom, bacon, liver, bacon, mushroom.

Brush the whole slightly with olive oil, arrange skewers in a heavy tin or oven-glass pie plate with handle of the skewers at the outside edge. Place in hot oven; turn after six minutes and when the bacon is crisp, mushrooms and livers golden brown, sprinkle with salt and pepper and freshly chopped chive and serve on the same plate. A decorative garnish is broiled tomatoes. Cut them in half, sprinkle with oil and chive, salt and pepper, and place watercress around the platter. This is one variety of the many possibilities of skewer dishes. Calves' liver, cubes of lamb, beef, or pork, all can be treated the same way, and served with any kind of vegetable. The gravy which is produced by the bacon, the fine liver, and mushroom juices should never be thickened. Pour hot over the meat. The celery-root salad recipe is on page 85.

THE THIRD MENU

Beet bouillon (hot)
topped with sour cream
Broiled chicken *farci*
Broiled Spanish onions
Oriental salad
Pear compote
Demi-tasse

For beet bouillon see Chapter 8, page 150.

For broiled chicken *farci.* After the chicken has had its usual cleaning it still needs grooming by rubbing outside and inside with lemon juice (as described on page 111). Then comes the under-the skin stuffing of parsley, rosemary, and a whiff of the liaison herb, chive, all finely cut and mixed with sweet butter, seasoned with salt and a *soupçon* of powdered ginger. Salt the inside of the chicken and rub what is left of the herbal stuffing and an additional piece of butter (size of a nut) deeply into the little crevices of the chicken. Protect the broiler with a few bacon strips attached to the chicken with small wooden skewers. Broil under low flame until bacon is crisp. Place for the last five minutes in the upper part of the oven, turned to 400° F. so that the inside is well done. Leave the gravy untouched.

For a small dinner party the broilers should be taken to the dining room sizzling hot, decorated with a few bouquets of watercress and served directly from broiler grid to the hot plates. On another broiling rack are placed the thick slices of Spanish onions (parboiled in sweet butter unseasoned) covered with seasoned sour cream. The seasonings for the sour cream are dill salt (if fresh dill is not available) and paprika. This is a rare combination and excellent with all broiled meats.

To make Oriental salad for four, cook one-half cup of unsoaked Carolina rice after frying it in a pan with one tablespoon of olive oil until slightly yellow. Add three tablespoons of water, cover tightly, cook on top of the range or in the oven. This takes longer in the oven but the result is better. Let cool and place in a salad bowl as the basis for the salad; use one pimiento, finely chopped; one-half cup fresh-cooked green peas; one cup string beans cut in short slices (cooked slightly underdone) seasoned with freshly grated white pepper and salt and sprinkled with sweet marjoram; one-half cup diced cooked carrots, seasoned with salt and pepper and minced parsley; six mushroom caps peeled, raw, cut in fine slices and sprinkled with salt and lemon juice; one-half cup cubes of cucumbers. Make herbal French dressing rather spicy. Use six chopped capers, two minced shallots, a dash of curry powder, a dash of ginger, and a dash of sugar. The salad must be very "hot" in appearance and texture but not spicy as to flavor.

The compote of pears is made with ripe pears halved and stewed in light white wine with some spices and sugar; then served cold.

THE FOURTH MENU

This menu was planned to exploit the lobster, by demonstrating the bouillon of lobster, lobster butter and cold lobster for all its worth, accompanied by various sauces which are congenial to the lobster without making it into salad. Therefore the demonstration turned out to be a kind of lobster orgy, relieved only by a sobering Romaine salad. This took place in a charming environment with the winter sun pouring into a spacious kitchen, on eager, gay young women. In the balancing of this luncheon the lobster weighed too heavy! There was enough for three ordinary meals. But I threw my conscience to the wind. When looking over an old menu of my ancestor's era, I found that a list of dishes which filled me with awe and remorse had only been the beginning of what they called a supper menu for the family table!

Back to the lobster. Before it earns its royal robes a formidable bouillon has to be prepared.

The bouillon—for two lobsters or four people:

2 Spanish onions	2 bay leaves crushed
4 carrots	1 teaspoon caraway seed
2 turnips	1 sprig wild marjoram
1 celery root	1 teaspoon mixed spice
1 parsley root and leaves	1 tablespoon of salt

Boil this mixture in three quarts of water for two hours. It should then be reduced to one and a half quarts. Strain it and bring it again to the boiling point when the two live lobsters are dipped into it. After the lobsters have turned red (fifteen minutes) the pot is set aside and the lobsters cool off with the bouillon. Then take the lobsters from their bouillon, cut in half, pick the meat from the shell and set aside. With the eggs and fat of the lobster the shell is pounded to smithereens and returned to the bouillon, to which has been added a quarter pound of fresh butter, and boiled again until the butter turns red orange on the surface The bouillon is strained and placed in the refrigerator until the red butter has grown stiff, when it is taken from the bouillon and placed separately in a bowl for further use.

The bouillon without the butter is most delicious to serve by itself, especially if sour cream is served with it. Therefore *the bouillon should not be used as a bisque if the next course will be lobster*. It really is an insult to both. The lobster plays a more important role if used separately from the bouillon. The butter is the basis for any *ragoût fin,* or a curried lobster, or lobster *côtelette,* or after all for a perfect bisque.

What we did at our lobster lesson was to serve a bisque using both bouillon and a part of this precious butter. Of course it was a meal in itself especially as tiny hot *piroshkis* (Russian biscuits) with herbal stuffing were served with it. Part of the lobsters were served hot with a Hollandaise sauce mixed with horseradish. The part which was served cold had a green mayonnaise (*sauce ravigote*). All was eaten with great enthusiasm.

The Romaine salad, sober and refreshing, really was to satisfy my feelings as the redeeming touch to so heavy a menu. The demi-tasse was a godsend.

Thus ended our lobster feast.
A confession and a warning!

THE FIFTH MENU

Vegetable bouillon
Saddle of lamb, Caucasian style
Parsley potatoes
Salade Topinambour
Cucumber with dill and sour cream
Sabayone

I used this for a luncheon lesson, yet it was a dinner menu. The vegetable bouillon was one of the rare elixirs which does not need any other support. It consisted of one bunch of carrots, four turnips, four unpeeled potatoes, one small head of cabbage, six stalks of leek (the white part), one tablespoon of caraway seed, three parsley roots, one cup of green dried peas, one cup of white beans, one-half cup of lentils, and two tablespoons of coarse salt, cooked in one gallon of water for five hours very slowly until it was reduced to two quarts, strained through a fine strainer and the bulk pressed down to get all the juices out without puréeing the bouillon. It was clear, strong, of a light brown, and when served a few drops of lemon juice were added and half a demi-tasse spoon of sherry. This bouillon can be served hot or cold with sweet or sour cream, or clear.

Saddle of lamb is the two-sided rack of a spring lamb. The butcher cut the ribs apart to the backbone and cut off some of the bare ribs. Between these the marinade was inserted as is described in Chapter 6, page 104. The already advocated slow-oven baking was used for this lamb too. In this the stuffing was protected by a blanket of bacon strips (of medium thickness, pinned to the meat by skewers), and the length of roasting time depended upon the poundage. For five pounds of lamb, three and one-half hours in unchanged temperature of 250° F. turned out a very successful roast. No basting is done. The juices flow naturally. The roast does not shrink and with a few tablespoons of sour cream added to the natural gravy this rack of lamb is an excellent roast.

Topinambour salad is made of what is known in this country as the Jerusalem artichoke. A knobby potato-like vegetable, it is of rare delicacy and not enough appreciated. The thoroughly brushed root is boiled unpeeled in mildly salted water until tender, cooled off and peeled and immediately sprinkled with lemon juice. The *topinambour* tastes best with a mild French dressing, to which some finely chopped lemon, thyme, and parsley are added. It makes a nice combination on a platter if surrounded by a wreath of watercress. For salad it usually is cut in round slices; for *hors d'œuvre* in cubes covered with a *tartare* sauce. As the class that day outnumbered the usual attendance we had to substitute another kind of salad of quick making.

To make cucumber salad fresh cucumbers are cut in cubes, seasoned with dill and sour cream and sprinkled with paprika. This has since become a favorite dish in the households of my pupils. It is most refreshing and in the northern countries very often served as *hors d'œuvre.*

Sabayone is a well-known and excellent dessert, a kind of milder and lighter eggnog. It is made of one-half cup of a very light white wine (the California sauterne will do) beaten in a double boiler with two egg yolks mixed with four teaspoons of sugar. This makes three glasses. The beating of the material should be started in the upper part of the boiler over hot, yet not boiling water. It will have fluffed high up when the water is boiling. Sprinkle the top with cinnamon or add a few drops of lemon juice before pouring into tall glasses.

THE SIXTH MENU

Bouillon of oyster plant
Guinea hen
Russian *kasha* (buckwheat groats)

Parsley-root salad
Compote of apricots

To make the bouillon of oyster plant for four, there really must be two bouillons to give the delicate and sensitive oyster plant extract, or rather its transparent purée, the right support. Barley is cooked with a few celery leaves and some parsley roots. When boiled to a light but substantial bouillon, it is strained and mixed with the bouillon of the oyster plant.

For four people, half a cup of pearl barley and the outer leaves of one celery and four parsley roots are cooked in one quart of water, to be reduced to one pint when added to the oyster plant bouillon.

One bunch of oyster plant is brushed and cooked in one quart of bouillon of one calf's foot, a handful of spinach, and the white of four leeks, all cooked down to one pint of liquid after straining. The seasoning is salt to taste (coarse salt preferred) and one teaspoon of lemon juice. This bouillon is very delicate and without making a cream soup of it one egg yolk with two tablespoons of heavy cream is a delectable addition. Combine the two bouillons and serve hot.

The guinea hen was marinated and stuffed, as in Chapter 6, page 118, wrapped in thin slices of bacon and treated as a slow-cooking roast in a low temperature oven for two and one-half hours. The gravy, very succulent, is smoothed with a few spoonfuls of sour cream or good sherry. The sour cream has been declared much better in character than the sherry for this particular use.

Russian *kasha* is known in the United States as coarse brown buckwheat groats, and can be bought in delicatessen stores in packages of one pound, with directions which can be followed exactly.

Parsley-root salad. Many of my pupils never suspected the parsley of having a root! The parsley which is used as the decorative or a wonderfully utilitarian herb has very tiny roots. It is the Italian coarse parsley which is used as a most aromatic herb for bouillons and stews, with the long and stout roots making it a vegetable and a salad of great delicacy. The roots are boiled unpeeled. It is easier to get the skin off when the root is cooked; it is then sprinkled immediately with lemon juice which keeps the root from getting dark. Cut in thin round slices, sprinkled generously with very finely cut parsley after the roots have stood half an hour in the usual herbal French dressing. Serve in a bowl with a circle of cubed red beets, treated with the dressing, and this surrounded by finely cut sorrel (in summertime).

The salad is served with herbal sandwiches of rye-krisp. Romaine salad is splendid with tiny celery-root cubes, bedded in the long leaves of the Romaine and treated with herbal French dressing.

Compote of apricots flavored with a dash of port wine is the gay finale to such a menu to keep the balance sheet correct.

THE SEVENTH MENU

Potato soup
Oysters in beer batter
Spinach *Impérial*
Black cherries

For potato soup see Chapter 8, page 154.

Oysters from the half shell on skewers, fried in a beer batter, was one of the Lenten dishes. The oysters were marinated with a very light mixture two hours before using. After the oysters were opened the mixture was applied immediately: finely cut chervil, the salad herbs, lemon juice, and shallots finely minced. The oysters were speared on skewers five inches long, and had invited as their company the glamorous mushroom, which got a dash of Tellicherry pepper and a dash of coarse salt. One dozen oysters and one dozen mushrooms were used to six skewers.

For the beer batter, one-eighth of a pound of sifted flour, one-half cup of light beer, one tablespoon of olive oil, the whites of two eggs, and salt and pepper to taste, were combined, the stiffly beaten egg whites added last. Each loaded skewer was dipped into the batter and fried in deep fat, very hot.

To judge the heat of the fat depends on what this fat consists of. Oil heats up very quickly and should never steam. Butter alone takes longer—first it bubbles and then it seems to be very inactive and this is the right moment for the frying. Lard has the same quality when being heated. Lard and butter mixed is a very pleasant-flavored cooking fat. Fresh butter cannot be used for deep-fat frying because of its milk residue, which too quickly browns the butter, often to the burning point. My frying butter is precooked, as I explain at the end of this chapter.

All deep-fat fried foods have to be taken from fat when golden blond, placed on a blotting paper or paper toweling and kept in a slightly heated oven. This dish was served very hot on a hot platter decorated with parsley and lemon slices. The handle of each skewer was topped with a paper *manchette*. Strip off the skewer with the fork when serving.

Spinach *Impérial* can be served with oysters, as may fresh peas. Spinach after its through cleaning is dry cooked, with hardly any water. It takes ten minutes to bring spinach to the tender point, then it should be sprinkled with salt, taken from the kettle, and placed on a board and made into four little bundles. Spread on each is herb butter well seasoned with salt, pepper, and a few drops of lemon juice. (Herbs: sweet marjoram, chervil, and chive finely minced—one tablespoon to one-eighth of a pound of spinach.) After the little bundles are rolled once over, they are placed on a tin platter in a warm oven. Before serving, another piece of the herb butter is placed on top of each one. This is an easy, delicious way of serving spinach.

Serve the black cherries with a dash of Cointreau.

THE EIGHTH MENU

Fish bouillon with croutons
Chicken, Balkan style
Rice
Salade printanière

For fish bouillon for six people use heads, backbones, and tails of mullets and southern mackerel, boiled with mixed spices, three bay leaves crushed, two large Spanish onions, two green peppers, one sprig of thyme, one sprig of wild marjoram, two turnips, a small celery root, one clove of garlic, and one tablespoon of coarse salt, in two quarts of water until the water is reduced to one quart. It is cooked until everything is demolished and can be strained like a purée of juices through a very fine strainer. One pound of sauerkraut is cooked for two hours and nothing but the juice from it is added to the fish bouillon. In case the bouillon is not quite clear, one whole egg should be broken, shell and all, and can be thrown into the strained and cooled bouillon. Then the pot is placed in the warmed oven where the egg will gather the remains of the strained vegetables. It is strained again and placed overnight in the refrigerator, when some of the fish oils will be stiffened on the top of the jellied bouillon. The oils are removed carefully, the bouillon heated and served very hot. Croutons of white bread, fried in butter and topped with grated cheese (Gruyère), are an agreeable addition.

To make the Balkan chicken for six people use two young chickens, weighing two and one-half pounds each. After being cleaned they are groomed by rubbing them inside and outside with lemon juice, holding half a lemon in the right hand. Some of the zesty lemon peel oil rubs itself into the chicken too. As little as this might seem to be, it has an influence on the ingredients of the sauce in which it is cooked. When cutting the chicken into six parts the giblets, liver, the upper part of the wings, the neck, and the back parts are set aside. For these undecorative pieces a pot of boiling water supplied with vegetables is waiting. These pieces make the chicken bouillon needed for the long sauce of the Balkan chicken. The bouillon has to be cooked first and the water reduced to almost half because this recipe demands the best for the main chicken in the casserole. The chicken waits for a while in the refrigerator. After an hour the bouillon will be at the point when the preparation of the chicken may begin.

First of all, one-half pound of bacon is cut finely and fried a golden brown, more golden than brown. Then three big finely cut Spanish onions (the Bermuda or sweet kind will do because after all there are no more Spanish onions coming in!) are added, until both are well acquainted—about fifteen minutes—then the chicken is added. When there need to be layers, each one is covered with bacon-onion mixture, sprinkled with salt, and covered with paprika until the chicken is comfortably established. Herb butter (rosemary, chervil, and parsley) the size of an egg is added on top of the chicken and the whole covered tightly and cooked very slowly on a low flame. Before closing the chicken pot one small piece of the vicious pepperoni (or red chili) is added.

After half an hour the chicken will have developed its juices, which must not be permitted to be reduced too far. One cup of the chicken bouillon is then added, and the chicken cooked another half hour. At this time one pound of freshly shelled green peas, one dessert spoon of coarse salt, and if needed some more of the bouillon are added, and simmered until the correct tenderness is reached and the peas done, but not overcooked, as this ruins the beauty of the dish. One cup of sweet cream and one teaspoon of paprika are mixed and added to the sauce, and all heated to just below the boiling point.

The salad is a mixed green spring salad with a simple herbal dressing.

THE NINTH MENU

Bouillon Impérial
Shad, *Sauce Soubise*
Parsley potatoes
Spring salad
The cake without flour

This demonstration was quite an occasion, the class *en parade.*

There was once an emperor of legendary age; his strength was waning—almost beyond help. But, like a fairy tale, help came. His Majesty's great chef was praying on his knees that he might be enlightened to create something that would prolong the life of his beloved emperor. The old emperor really was a shameless eater, and it was he who broke the precedent of the relentless etiquette decreed when the Hapsburgs were kings of Spain. It had been the custom that when the most alluring courses were set before the guests, as soon as they started to eat the plates disappeared with lightning speed and others were there instead. It was most exasperating. This emperor even went so far as to give the first example of taking the little chicken or squab legs in his fingers to gnaw them down to the bones. The shocked flunkies rapidly presented the golden fingerbowl so that all these *grandes dames* and *grands seigneurs* could clean their fingers before the next course was served.

The old chef's prayers were answered and he created *Bouillon Impérial* which made the blood tingle again in the emperor's cheeks. To use the chef's own words, "Everything is in this bouillon which creeps, flies, runs, or swims."

Thus into my cooking pot went a matronly fat and round pigeon, some river trout, several calves' feet, also a shin of beef, a deer's liver, and instead of some crawfish I had to choose a lobster. This combination cooked six hours, unsalted, with two sprigs of borage, ten finely minced shallots, one sprig of thyme and a little bag of mixed herbs—I used the omelet herbs which were a fine addition. This bouillon simmered down to a wonderful deep brown elixir, and when served in a cup no larger than a demi-tasse it certainly made the blood tingle in the cheeks of my pupils, too.

The shad. There were two marvels of big shad with their noble silver coats, for our class. The coats, of course, had to be skinned off because the *Sauce Soubise* was the intended new spring wrap for our shad. First they were marinated in light white wine, and were resting, in reality, on laurels—bay leaves. There were the four-spice powder and three of the fine herbs—rosemary, thyme, and chive (garlic and onions were excused for the shad). There was winter savory and fennel of the robust herbs. The shad was steamed fifteen minutes in this marinade after the fish underwent a slight rubbing in of salt, Sarawak pepper, and lemon.

Sauce Soubise is one of those grand sauces which is almost classic, yet which permits variation in its flavors. The basic element is the Bermuda or sweet onion. For one shad (three pounds) use one onion chopped very fine, mixed with six ounces of butter (fresh, unsalted) to a thick purée, and with one cup of finely cut chervil, half a cup of finely cut parsley, and salted and peppered to taste. The cooked shad was lying expectantly on the big hot platter to receive the green cloak which was this sauce.

Spring salad brought a novelty to the table. I discovered in the market my favorite spring vegetable—the very young *favi* (Italian), (*fèves*, French; broad beans, English); a regular *primeur*. My pupils had to take them not only from the shell but from their hull where they were bedded, the greenest, spring-like crisp little beans; and thus they received the honor place in the salad bowl, still raw, surrounded by the young, tender leaves of Boston lettuce and of the never failing watercress, and the one unsurpassed French herbal dressing with tarragon as the favorite flavor.

The cake without flour. And here I hand to the world one of my most cherished possessions, the recipe of the cake of my childhood, the solemn cake for all solemn occasions. As forever, really great things are the most uncomplicated, the simplest. So is this cake. Just hazelnuts, those superb little nuts which nature let grow in a dainty cradle in the midst of all summer shrubs—a little hard to get like all good things. (How I love hazelnuts

—for me they are still the finest of all nuts!) One has to open two pounds of hazelnuts to grate the one pound which is needed for this cake, and when grated they are mixed with one pound of sugar which is beaten first to a golden yellow clarity with ten yolks of fresh eggs. Yes, beaten by hand to get the right texture. In this mixture the hazelnuts are imbedded and softened by twelve whites of eggs beaten to a stiff froth. And this is all—no baking powder, nothing to further increase its goodness. The cake pan is brushed with olive oil and powdered with sifted flour, the cake mixture poured into the pan, and baked in a low oven (300° F.) without being disturbed. To make sure, try with a knitting needle and if there is no dough clinging to it the cake is done. Cool off the oven; remove the cake from the pan when entirely cooled. Slice through with a sharp knife making two layers (this might be postponed to the following morning). Have whipping cream (without sugar) ready to place between the two layers and on top of the cake; serve cool. This is food for gods!

THE TENTH MENU

Silotka (Russian herring)—*hors d'œuvre*
Tenderloin of pork

Asparagus
Noodles with Parmesan

Russian herring. This was a daring *hors d'œuvre* to serve my group because the Russian herring is not that kind of *hors d'œuvre* which bashfully conceals its proletarian background in some trembling colored jelly or in frosted cups behind an indefinable condiment as a so-called seafood cocktail. The herring is proletarian; he marches in great masses or swims in great masses, yet is welcomed by rich and poor. Nations thrive on herrings —nations around the North and Baltic Seas—and there is never a day in the year in Russia that *silotka* is not always on the table and always *au naturel.* Changes of governments or creeds never affect the herring. Tsars or Stalins, the people will not be without it.

I smuggled my herrings into the kitchen without being suspected. I hid them in a milk bath, heavily covered until the moment when they appeared skinned in slender fillets, protected by watercress and lemon slices, on the table. There were some who tried to ignore the modest appearance of this *hors d'œuvre;* not for long, the herring conquered. I really wanted it myself so badly, having denied myself this most refreshing salty morsel to which I had been accustomed for many years! The simple forthright taste of a good herring beats all other *hors d'œuvre,* most of which are so painstakingly composed and mixed. Herring has the vitamins of the codfish, and lacks the gout-producing proteins of caviar.

Tenderloin of pork. I realized that I was stepping down somewhat in my menu from the heights of selected foods, but I wanted just to demonstrate that tenderloin of pork should be in the same class as turkey; and a latecomer hurriedly adding to her plate some of the sliced roast exclaimed, "What an exquisite turkey!" In the kitchen the roast is taken from the marinade (see Chapter 6, page 107) and the marinade brushed off the tenderloin, leaving it, however, between the ribs. It was then rubbed lightly with caraway seed and sweet marjoram where the top fat had been removed, adding anchovy butter (unsalted butter mixed with anchovy paste or plain anchovies freed from their sea salt by soaking in water for twenty-four hours). Thus the tenderloin needed salting only on the bottom. It was baked by the slow-oven system in three and one-half hours to a juicy tenderness. A few tablespoons of cream completed the gravy.

Asparagus was steamed (the asparagus tied in a bunch has to stand upright in the water with its heads above the boiling water, yet in the steam). By this method the stalks are done the same time that the heads are tender without being cooked to a purée. The water was salted only when the asparagus had cooked ten minutes. I let it cool off, serving it as a cold dish with a kind of *vinaigrette* sauce, which is spiced vinegar boiled down, mixed with some white or red wine and some finely cut shallots, tarragon, parsley, and a few drops of lemon juice. Finely cut capers without their vinegar is a nice addition to this. Cold asparagus takes kindly to a *vinaigrette*—the sauce must be very cold.

The noodles with Parmesan were of the broadest variety, just cooked in salted water and rinsed with cold water when done, and somewhat dried before throwing them into sizzling butter to be browned slightly. After removing to a hot serving dish, they were covered thickly with Parmesan cheese and the mixing done on each individual plate to prevent the sticking of the cheese to the noodles.

THE ELEVENTH MENU

Bouillon of Florence fennel
Leg of domestic spring lamb with pineapple stuffing
Wild rice
Romaine salad, anchovy dressing
Compote of apricots

The bouillon of Florence fennel was made with two calves' feet cooked the day before and permitted to jell. Next day the fat was removed and set aside. (The Florence fennel is the root of the ferny green herb.) The fennel was washed and cut in thick slices and the stems placed with the leaves altogether in two quarts of water. One-half tablespoon of salt was added and four ounces of fresh unsalted butter. As the *finocchio,* or fennel, developed its own fine-flavored bouillon it was reduced to half. The fennel was cooked in the pot until it fell to pieces, strained and mixed with calf's-foot bouillon with two ounces of fresh butter and a handful of finely cut chervil. Before serving, a few drops of lemon juice and a half teaspoon of sour cream were placed in each cup. This soup is the perfect hot summer-day soup and can be served cold if, instead of butter, heavy cream is used when the bouillons are ready to be mixed. The cream should not be boiled.

Leg of spring lamb. This was a very slender young leg and had to be treated accordingly. The marinade of the spring lamb differs from the winter marinade. It is much lighter. Onions and only a fragment of garlic were mixed with rosemary, thyme, and bay leaf for the marinade. The leg was freed of its top fat, and four pocket-like incisions were made between skin and meat for the marinade. After twelve hours the marinade was removed from the pockets only, the lamb seasoned with salt and pepper, and slices of fresh pineapple and butter the size of a nut, were put in each pocket. Large strips of bacon pinned to the top with skewers held them down. The roast was placed in a 250° F. oven for two hours.

Wild rice, a strictly American product, was cooked in its usual way (following the clear directions always given on the boxes of rice) with a small addition of a few cumin seeds and one-half teaspoon sweet marjoram to add zest.

Romaine salad. Into the French dressing was beaten one teaspoon anchovy paste. No salt was added. The dressing was imbedded in each leaf.

Apricot compote was mixed with roasted almonds and a dash of Cointreau.

THE TWELFTH MENU

Cream of cucumber soup—cold
Rye-krisp with watercress butter
Sturgeon Muscovite
Spring carrots
New green peas
New potatoes, parsley butter
French endive salad, French dressing
Canned figs

For the cream of cucumber soup recipe see Chapter 8, page 152.

Sturgeon Muscovite. I discovered in our market the sturgeon—this fish from the most northern waters, the fish from the Volga, the precious sturgeon, which produces the rare caviar eggs. I was greatly excited because of all the fish in Russia I adored sturgeon. There were memories of the past when sturgeons were exhibited in all their gigantic proportions on ice blocks surrounded by wreaths of flowers and greens, in the center of the big dining rooms of big hotels in Russia. Very barbaric indeed, but oh, so promising.

One steak of sturgeon, for two, was marinated in our demonstration for two hours in a mixture of one bay leaf, two shallots, minced, a dash of thyme, a little lemon peel, one tablespoon olive oil, one-half tablespoon lemon juice, and one-fourth teaspoon freshly grated pepper. One cup of white wine, two cups of water, and one tablespoon of herb vinegar were added to the marinade and boiled for one hour, reducing the amount of liquid to one pint. It was then strained and returned to the saucepan, one tablespoon of coarse salt added, and the fish steak placed in the bouillon, where it was steamed for fifteen minutes, covered.

It is important not to overcook the sturgeon because

instead of getting soft it gets tough, just as steak toughens in overcooking. Of course if there is fresh caviar available, it is the logical company for sturgeon. Black or pressed caviar is not used this way. It is a different product. If the sturgeon is served with a sauce of fresh horseradish (Chapter 4, page 71) and surrounded by mild carrots and peas the combination is delicious. If to be served cold, it is left in the bouillon, the bouillon forming a jellied rim around it. A *macédoine* of vegetables and a *tartare* sauce or *vinaigrette* can accompany it. When I demonstrated the sturgeon it was a surprise to all of my pupils—I might say a shock, they never having tasted a fish which produced such steaky meat, without any bones. It was a curious adventure. The swordfish might be kin to sturgeon, but it lacks the fine quality and texture of sturgeon.

French endive salad completed this menu. French dressing, with chervil the dominating herb, was delicious on this delicate salad.

These twelve menus from among my demonstrations are examples of perfect cooking adventures, and were a happy satisfaction, because all of my pupils looked forward to each lesson with live interest and expectation. They discovered for themselves how things ought to taste without being forced into stereotyped recipes. It was fascinating for them and for me to study the various shades of cooking—the great individualities of food, and its nuances. Cooking never will be a science; it is a flexible art, and varies with the mood of our own tastes. But the foundation which flavor and shades can affect depends always upon the ingredients with which we treat our foods. The freshness of the foods must be respected in every way, not solely because of the result to our palate but as the ultimate necessity for our health. We can prevent all kinds of disagreeable symptoms in skin, eyes, hair, and nails, which might be caused not necessarily by a food allergy, but by the way in which the foods had been prepared.

There are kitchen odors so stimulating they make our mouths water, and there are kitchen odors which kill all our joy of eating. The cause of the latter can be avoided. Once I possessed a very haughty little dog; he was one of the rare Pekinese which, like a wise old aristocrat and philosopher, was an epicure, and he could not be deceived. When I prepared food the dog always came into the kitchen, sitting quietly with eyes getting bigger and nostrils wider. With the food in front of him the tiny dog would first look at me with almost smiling eyes, and after each bite nod with satisfaction. Once a neighbor passed by, knocked at my door, and asked if I were about to have a banquet—with the fragrance that came out of the kitchen window. "It's a dog's banquet," I laughed. "Come in and taste." Indeed I could not cook anything which would not be a joy to my own senses, either in smell or in taste. It does not cost more to cook good things and it is so much more fun. Simple bread and butter—there is nothing more delectable if not only the bread but also the butter is fresh as new cream.

Good ingredients also simplify the *cuisine*. The cook must know how to use precooked fresh butter instead of the fresh butter. This warning about how to use butter in cooking should be in the first paragraph of my book, yet let it be near the last so that it may linger in the reader's memory. Butter for frying, deep or shallow, has to be freed first of all of its milk residue by boiling. Five or ten pounds or more should be bought when butter prices are lowest, because boiled butter keeps indefinitely if put away in earthen or crockery pots topped with heavy lids. The process of boiling butter is most simple. The butter must simmer slowly in a high narrow pot. When it bubbles, a handful of cornmeal is thrown in, and the butter simmered for two more hours. It finally quiets down and its delicate fat appears a light golden color on top. It is easily strained; the fat substances are clear above the milk residues, which are heavy and have gathered as a bulk on the bottom. Thus the butter is cleared of all the influences which could spoil its goodness and spoil the food for which butter is indispensable. The milk residue is very tasty and can be used for cookies or sauces immediately. For cake-making, boiled butter is of great satisfaction. And frying with boiled butter eliminates the spattering of grease which comes with lard or other fats.

After all has been said about the Fine and Robust Herbs, their importance, their distinction, and their characteristics, I have condensed their use to the simplest and clearest formula: the Fine Herbs are an addition, and, when applied to already cooked foods, emphasize this addition; foods topped with fine herbs, mixed with gravies, sauces, with oil or butter, reach a last delicate effect. Robust Herbs develop their aromatic and influential qualities only when cooking with the foods from the beginning, in boiling, roasting, or stewing; after their work has been done they should be discarded, and the bouillon, the gravy, or the sauce should be strained clear of the bulk.

CHAPTER TEN

How to Make a Family Herb Garden

ONE DAY IN LATE OCTOBER I stood in the midst of a five-acre herb garden between long rows of perennials, still green. There were chive, pot marjoram, winter savory, the French and English thymes, sage with its pebbled, gray-green leaves, the crisp-leaved mints, the lemon balm and the charming little bushes of rosemary grown to eighteen inches or more in height. The first frost had come and gone. All that was left of the summer savory and the many varieties of basil that had been the garden's crown of color, form, and fragrance—sweet, curly, lettuce-leaved basils, tall, decorative, purple basils, and the sacred basil of India—were a few magnificent plants left for seed. Long empty spaces waited for next year. Basil, summer savory, and sweet marjoram are the important annuals in the big group of herbs belonging to the *Mint Family.*

The umbel-flowered group belonging to the *Parsley Family* are mostly annuals—so many of them already gone—chervil, caraway, and coriander, but crisp shoots of finely divided aromatic leaves had sprung up from the roots of dill and fennel, and the Italian parsley was as green as ever.

Looking out over these mature plants, or the spaces where they had stood, it was easy to understand why authorities say that a space six-by-ten feet will grow enough of the better and more important herbs for kitchen use for a small family. A few rows of twenty feet in the garden may grow to a small profitable business.

The herb garden must have plenty of sun but, in locating it, consideration should be given to its nearness to the kitchen. This will save many steps. Furthermore, in dry weather most of the plants will have to be watered, and under all circumstances these precious little plants should be grown under the caring hands and eyes of the home gardener.

From the very start it also should be understood that all perennials should be grown on one side, arranged so that the taller ones do not overshadow the smaller ones. The perennials have to stay in their original location for longer than a year, therefore special care has to be taken in the preparation of the soil. It is well also to plant the thick-leaved varieties requiring least moisture—sage, thyme, winter savory, and marjoram—in one part of the bed, and those that need more frequent watering in another part.

To arrive at satisfactory results the herb bed should be plowed or spaded to a depth of ten to fifteen inches, bone meal and well-rotted manure worked in, and the soil pulverized to the full depth. It is most essential that at all times the soil be thoroughly cultivated, freed from weeds, and, in case of drought, the plants well watered. This is necessary for the tiny seeds and fine roots of *thyme, marjoram, winter savory, and rosemary.* The seeds of perennials are often started indoors in a sunny window.

Annuals are started from seed each year. It also should be remembered that herbs which are the weedy kind should not annoy other garden plants, and therefore not be permitted to form more seed than is required for replanting.

A number of herbs can be started by growing the seeds in their garden beds, thinning the seedlings only after they become well established. These are chervil, parsley, dill, and summer savory. Others can be started in early spring in shallow boxes in a sunny window, or in a hotbed or cold frame. *Enough seedlings for a beginner's herb garden can be started in half a dozen cigar boxes but they must have sun and must not be allowed to dry out.* Although most of the annuals are grown from seed, *the mints, tarragon, and chive* are propagated by divisions and cuttings; with *sage, savory and thyme,* the layering is often adopted as the easiest method of propagating them successfully.

For the family herb garden on a plot of six-by-ten feet, the following herbs are recommended:

Annuals: basil, summer savory, chervil, parsley.

Biennials: dill.

Perennials: mints, marjoram, rosemary, sage, chive, tarragon, thyme.

Basil is one of the most popular kitchen herbs, useful in many ways, in fact, indispensable. Of the basils, the sweet basil is preferable for kitchen use, while the lettuce-leaved variety is grown for the quality of its leaves, which keep their aroma when dried. Basils are annuals, easy to start, and if tops are pinched out to within three or four inches from the ground, two or more crops can be harvested for drying. Fresh basil for winter use can be provided by potting garden plants, or better, by starting new seedlings in September and transplanting them to pots or boxes. Basil is decorative; the plants are about eight inches high and should be set twelve to fourteen inches apart.

Summer savory is a slender annual, not over twelve

inches tall, belonging to the mint family, and found occasionally as a naturalized plant on dry soil in the Middle West. Seed can be started in hotbeds, or planted outdoors in early spring, five or six to the inch, in rows as close as can be cultivated, and thinned to twelve or fourteen inches apart. Close cutting develops a compact, symmetrical plant. Summer savory is a traditional herb abroad, and has been used for over two thousand years. It is indispensable with green vegetables and in soups made of dry beans, peas, or lentils.

Chervil, an annual, belongs to the parsley family. In planting take five or six seeds to each hill, making the hills eight inches apart. Chervil is one of the finest herbs but, though belonging to the parsley family, it is much more subtle, and is one of the most cherished salad herbs. It therefore belongs to the group of fine herbs.

Parsley need not be grown in the family herb garden, as it can be so easily secured at the market. But if desired it should be planted exactly like chervil.

Dill is a biennial plant from the Mediterranean part of Europe. It has a resemblance to the wild carrot with leaves much finer, almost fern-like. Dill seeds are most popular for pickling, but amazingly little known in this country are the green leaves. There is nothing finer than those finely chopped leaves and they add tremendously to the flavor of the *cuisine.* If desired to have seeds the first season, the plants should be started indoors and early in spring set ten to fifteen inches apart.

The mints, spearmint and peppermint, are grown for flavoring. Mints grow best in moist, rich loam, and partly shaded. They need watching, belonging to the seedy kind; their spreading, however, can be checked by renewing the bed every few years. They are perennials and are propagated by cutting and dividing. Mints are too well-known to require comment as to their use.

Sweet marjoram is the pet herb of the kitchen. Its seeds are very small and therefore are sown indoors in early spring in specially prepared soil. It is a perennial but is treated often as an annual, especially in the northern part of this country. Sweet marjoram can be easily potted and grown indoors. This herb with its fine flavor improves the taste of soups, vegetables, and roasts.

Rosemary, the herb of old legends, is one of the most enchanting, with an almost holy fragrance. It belongs to the select group of fine herbs. To have grown rosemary potted or in the herb bed is a noble addition. It is a lovely stately plant and grows to two feet or more in height. Strangely, it does best in poor, light, rather limy soil. It is a perennial in mild climates, yet needs protection in the northernmost states. Plants are often taken indoors for the winter. Easily propagated by cutting and dividing, it is generally sown from seed. Its addition to stuffing for fowl and veal, and to salads and sauces, means a good deal, and it is delicious in drinks.

Sage is probably the most domesticated herb. It is a perennial and the seed should be sown in early spring about two to the inch, in rows, twelve to fourteen inches apart. Its use is widespread and needs no further comment.

Chive is a perennial and belongs to the onion family, with its onion-like flavor less pungent, very delicate and free of what one would call the aftermath of onions. It is well established in its everyday use and for many foods. Chive grows six to eight inches in height, and is easily propagated by dividing the clumps at least every third year.

Tarragon is an aristocrat among herbs, giving foods great distinction. Related to southernwood, it is much finer and milder. A perennial, it is a bushy plant with very fine leaves, up to two or three feet in height, propagated by cutting and dividing. Dry, poor, warm soil is preferable and the plants have to be protected during the winter. It has a variety of uses, but satisfaction depends on understanding how to use it in foods and to combine it with other herbs. Tarragon belongs to the select group of the fine herbs, used in salads, omelets, dressings, sauces, etc.

Thyme, a bushy perennial, grows eight to ten inches in height. Of all thymes, the common thyme is the most useful for kitchen use. Its seed is so tiny that it is best planted indoors and transplanted eighteen inches apart in rows, in rich moist soil. If grown vigorously, thyme will produce several crops during the summer. It winters well if covered with straw. The narrow-leaved thymes are the most preferable and most aromatic. Its kitchen use is of great variety, especially when combined with other herbs; it also is delicious in drinks.

These twelve herbs are indeed the indispensable ones among the thirty culinary herbs and varieties that are found in the complete herb gardens or farms. The planting and using of herbs will give to the everyday *cuisine* a zest not only welcome to break the usual monotony, but to help the digestive juices, which is an important factor in the family's health.

THE HERB BOX

The size of the box in which to grow the mature herb plants is immaterial, except that it should be at least eight inches deep and of a length that will fit under the window where it is to be kept. A layer of broken stones about an inch in thickness should be spread in the bottom of the box to allow any surplus water to drain out.

A compost of the following, one-fourth part decomposed cow manure, one-fourth part leaf mold, and one-half good loam top soil, is placed in the box. To this add in proportion not more than two ounces of commercial fertilizer to half a bushel of soil.

The following plants make a good bouquet: summer savory, sweet marjoram, basil, chive, rosemary, thyme, and chervil.

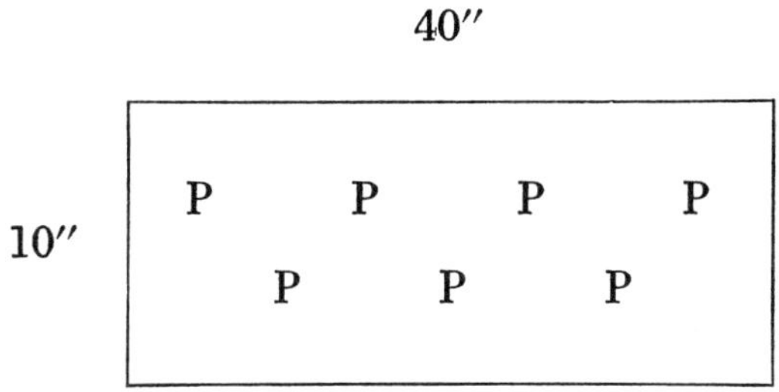

40″

10″

P P P P

P P P

The plants, as indicated by the P's, should be eight inches apart.

In the box the plants should not be crowded too much, and should be watered twice a week or oftener if the soil is found to be drying out. Do not forget there must always be sunshine on the box. It is best placed in a southwest window.

INDEX

Index

Index

Index

Index